O _ _ _
SMART
CROWD

How crowdsourcing is
changing the world
one idea at a time

Simon Hill
Alpheus Bingham

V2.06 January 2021

To my wife and kids, who are the inspirational force behind everything I do. Everything is possible to those who dare to believe they can. We can all have wings and were born to fly as high as our minds allow us. We can all change the world one idea at a time.

Simon

To the InnoCentive Solvers who NEVER cease to amaze me. Over and over again, we have posted challenges when I thought to myself, "no one is gonna have anything useful to say on this obscure topic." And, over and over again, the solvers not only have something useful but something brilliant, something unique, and something profound to contribute. Thank you for providing me with many years of renewed faith in the human creativity and genius distributed in every culture, every continent, every clime and every generation around the world.

Alph

Foreword

Have you ever participated in a brainstorming session that resulted in walls covered with Post-it® notes? Afterwards, did you wonder if there was a more efficient and powerful way to innovate?

One thing we've learned over the past several decades is that innovation is rarely found by sifting through thousands of ideas. Instead it is driven by the quality of the questions we ask.

This is Challenge-Driven Innovation®.

The starting point is an important issue, problem, challenge, or opportunity that if solved would have a big impact for the organization. The need precedes the solution. Most innovation efforts fail at this first step.

Solving the wrong problem will always lead to irrelevant or unimportant solutions. And not framing the problem properly can prevent you from seeing viable and valuable solutions. Taking time to ask the right question the right way leads to clarity.

This is an important step, but it is only the first step.

Once your challenge is clearly defined, now it is time to look for solutions. Unfortunately, our past experiences limit our ability to see different and potentially better futures because they put blinders on us.

When members of an innovation team are cut from the same cloth, although you may find solutions quickly, they will almost certainly be incremental in natural and derivatives of past ideas.

Breakthroughs require diverse experiences and backgrounds.

1

As I like to say, rocket science isn't always rocket science. If you have a hundred rocket scientists trying to solve an aerospace problem and you still can't find a solution, adding one more rocket scientist to the mix probably will not make a shred of difference. But looking elsewhere—like lingerie and Hollywood— can lead to better solutions (yes, NASA looked to these industries for some of their innovations).

This is where crowdsourcing excels.

Whether you are asking an internal group of employees or an external network, crowdsourcing allows people with a wide range of experiences to participate. And an added bonus to this approach is that people are working in parallel. By looking for solutions at the same time you not only increase the likelihood of success, but you also reduce the timeframe needed to find solutions.

For the past 15 years, I have witnessed the incredible breakthroughs that InnoCentive has uncovered through their incredible 400,000-person strong solver network. They have helped make huge advances in medicine, space travel, oil spill clean-up, and so much more. But this is just the tip of the iceberg. By connecting the brightest minds with the biggest problems, this crowd can and will generate the most valuable and impactful solutions.

These are exciting times for innovation. It's time to innovate the way you innovate and tap into One Smart Crowd.

Stephen Shapiro

Author of Invisible Solutions and Best Practices are Stupid

AUTHOR

I am Alpheus Bingham

I live in the US

I am a scientist and entrepreneur

Along with my partners
I had the idea for Innocentive

Ian Smyth 2020

My name is Alpheus Bingham

In 2011 together with co-author Dwayne Spradlin, I wrote 'The Open Innovation Marketplace' (Pearson Publishing, FT Press 2011). It takes the reader on a journey through all aspects of open innovation and the opportunity it presents to create value in the challenge driven enterprise. In the Afterword of that book we closed with this thought;

> "We observe and facilitate unbelievably inspiring stories of the power of crowds to do everything from accelerating industrial research, to imagining new business opportunities, to accelerating cures for neglected diseases. These stories may well be the basis of the next book."

It feels somewhat like the fulfillment of a promise therefore to bring this set of stories together in this book. Many of these stories are taken from a collection of blogs entitled "I am a Solver" wherein the InnoCentive Solvers told their stories, as well as via other numerous emails and exchanges over the years. These stories have been told countless times at MIT, at TEDMED, at the Economist conferences and beyond, all around the world. And now, through this book they will continue to be told. As they should. They impress not just the audiences but continue to impress me. And it's not just the examples of those who have already been awarded bounties for their solutions. We continue to try and understand how our solver community is collectively smart, how each member is a solution waiting to happen. Each one is another story waiting to be told. To all the InnoCentive Solvers, let me say once again, "thank you, you are truly incredible."

AUTHOR

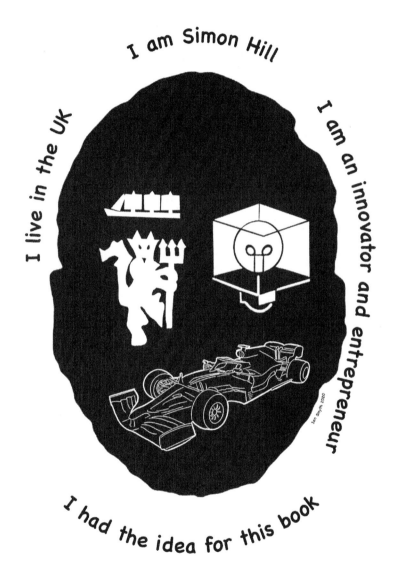

I am Simon Hill

I live in the UK

I am an innovator and entrepreneur

I had the idea for this book

My name is Simon Hill

In 2011, as Dr. Alpheus Bingham ("Alph") was writing The Open Innovation Marketplace, I was just embarking on my entrepreneurial journey as the founder of Wazoku (www.wazoku.com). My life could have taken any number of directions at that time. I had a number of different ideas I was playing with, but the idea behind Wazoku was the one that kept going round and round in my head, and the one I ultimately opted to invest the past 9 years of my life in developing. Every new innovation started its life as an idea. An idea that was seeking to address a perceived market need in some way. An idea that the inventor or innovator had enough conviction in to invest time, energy, money, sweat, tears and more.

In 2020, my entrepreneurial journey took another big step, as Wazoku acquired the assets of InnoCentive. Having met Alph during 2019, it has been a hugely exciting next step for the businesses we both started. I feel a great responsibility for the next phase of the Wazoku & InnoCentive journey and am excited for where the combination of our entrepreneurial ideas can go from here.

At the heart of both businesses is an unswerving belief in the innate creativity of people and that the best solutions often come from the unlikeliest of sources. We observe, that despite the data rich world we live in, we still know very little about the skills and motivations of most people, and still tend to operate in very confined, homogenous bubbles when it comes to problem solving and innovation. We are setting about trying to change this. Creating a new toolkit for identifying, defining and then solving problems, bringing together diverse and creative minds from around the world, to solve problems more efficiently and effectively than we have ever seen.

Both Alph and I share the same passion to bring the stories in this book to the world. Beyond the fact that this is also something Alph mused on in the closing of his prior book. Beyond the pleasing symbolism of us co-authoring this alongside Wazoku taking over the business Alph co-founded. These stories are living proof of the things we often read about great innovation successes. Innovation thrives with diversity (in all forms), where ideas are allowed to flow, and where the need is well defined. As we say at Wazoku, at the intersection of People, Ideas and Problems. I am delighted to share this incredible set of stories with you and hope you find them as fascinating and inspiring as I do.

Open Innovation:
The long tail of innovation

Henry Chesbrough is a professor at the Haas Business School, UC Berkeley and the originator of concept of open innovation. In his 2003 book, Open Innovation – The New Imperative for Creating and Profiting from Technology (Harvard Business Press), Chesbrough discussed the need for a more distributed, more participatory, more decentralized approach to innovation, based on the observed fact that useful knowledge today is widely distributed, and no company, no matter how capable or how big, could innovate effectively on its own. He observed that open innovation is a more profitable way for businesses to innovate, because it can reduce costs, accelerate time to market, increase differentiation in the market, and create new revenue streams for the company.

As the father of open innovation, it seems fitting to use Chesbrough's definition of open innovation to frame it for you:

"Open innovation is the use of purposive inflows and outflows of knowledge to accelerate internal innovation, and expand the markets for external use of innovation, respectively."

However, even before Chesbrough wrote his important book on the subject, an early wave of innovative thinkers had begun to bring the idea of open innovation to the market. One of the earliest firms in the market was InnoCentive Inc. The idea for InnoCentive (www.innocentive.com) came to Dr. Alpheus

Bingham and Aaron Schacht in 1998 while working at the pharmaceutical giant Eli Lilly and Company, during a brainstorming session exploring the application of the Internet to business. InnoCentive was then launched in 2001.

"We imagined during this brainstorming session a web-based system that would attract hundreds or even thousands of minds to tackle a problem in organic syntheses, more effectively exploring the vast domain of solution space. In later days, as we talked about this "molecule.com," we came more fully to three realizations: there will always be someone smarter outside of your team or organization; getting a diverse range of fresh perspectives is key to effective problem solving; and asking the right question in the right way is critical to eliciting the answers you need. These went on to be central pillars of InnoCentive." (Dr. Alpheus Bingham, InnoCentive co-founder)

As a pioneer of open innovation as a service, InnoCentive has helped global corporations, governments, and nonprofits across a range of industries to embrace the power of the crowd and has successfully solved thousands of innovation challenges.

There are a number of important tenants that underpin open innovation:

- Not all the smart people work for your company, so you must find and tap into the knowledge and expertise of bright individuals outside of your company.
- External R&D can create significant value: internal R&D is needed to claim some portion of that value
- You don't have to originate the research to profit from it.
- The firms that make the best use of internal and external ideas will outperform.
- Profit from others' use of your IP, and buy others' IP whenever it advances your business model.

As Bill Joy, former CEO Sun Microsystems once observed, "… most of the smart people work for someone else" (source: Lakhani KR, Panetta JA (2007). The Principles of Distributed Innovation. 2. MIT Press. SSRN 1021034), in a globalized world with an increasingly mobile and discerning employment market, the best talent (no matter how awesome your internal team) almost certainly works for someone else. You may raise an eyebrow to this, and we are absolutely not questioning the amazing people inside your organization, for sure you have amazing subject matter experts with PhDs, MBAs, and more. But the emergence of Open Talent business models (InnoCentive, Upwork, Freelancer etc.) offers a different future of work than the traditional 9-5 job and increasing numbers are adopting this form of work. However, there is another paradigm also at play. Consider this analogy from Amazon, "more than half of Amazon's book sales come from outside its top 130,000 titles" (Wired, 2004).

The long tail is real and is important. InnoCentive's business model takes the long tail of innovation and turns it into a competitive advantage for its customers. The volume in the tail will always exceed the volume in the head (see fig.1 below) This is the central tenet to the InnoCentive model.

As a customer once put it "we have technical superiority in the individuals in our organisation and we can compete individually with any of you, but we can't compete with all of you!" The InnoCentive long tail provides access to a global crowd, that over the years since 2001 has grown to more than 400,000 inquisitive minds, on a quest to unlock solutions to the world's most critical challenges. One Smart Crowd.

This book is a celebration of some of the stories from a subset of the incredible minds who are part of the One Smart Crowd (a self selected community registered on the InnoCentive.com website), all of who do not work for the companies for which they solved a complex innovation challenge. Each found their way to be part of this global community through some path in their life, some aspect of their curiosity, mindset, interests or other.

This is the story behind each of them and gives an insight into this hugely powerful, hugely important, often underestimated and frequently mis-understood long tail of global inventors and innovators.

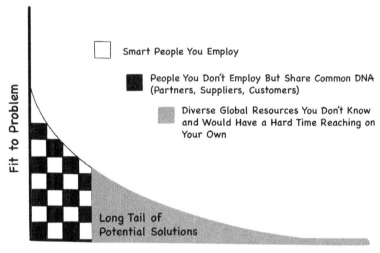

fig.1   Universe of Potential Problem Solvers

A problem shared is a problem solved.

What does it take to solve a problem? Is it simply that eureka moment? How much does your background, education, upbringing, the way you process information come into play? Is problem solving always collaborative, or can it be worked out in a silo?

No matter what business you are in, there is always an opportunity to work better, faster or smarter. There is scope to pivot, change or add value. There is always a challenge to overcome. But what happens when these challenges can't be solved by your own experts, or within your own network?

A book by Frans Johansson brought to light what's known as 'The Medici Effect', the notion that most breakthrough innovation results from the intersection of ideas from people of different fields, cultures and backgrounds. Modern day Medici Effect is amplified by the internet and social media offering 24/7 connectivity to anyone with access. Our world today, is one where you can connect and collaborate with people you never knew existed, to solve problems and generate ideas to drive your business forward. That's crowdsourcing. That's open innovation. And it's what companies like InnoCentive and Wazoku specialize in.

Open innovation enables us to find people (academics, experts, specialists, and SME's, etc.) from around the world that we don't currently know and work with them to accentuate the strength of our existing workforce. It empowers us to problem solve and view needs and problems from a different perspective, by combining different locations, cultures, backgrounds and areas of expertise.

InnoCentive is the global pioneer in crowdsourced innovation, helping organizations solve their important technology, science, business, AI and data challenges by connecting them with a global network of expert problem solvers. It's these solvers that have inspired this book and it's their tales of innovation that we're excited to share.

"To develop a complete mind: Study the art of science; study the science of art. Learn how to see. Realize that everything connects to everything else."
Leonardo Di Vinci

There are many types of people in the world and many types of problems that need solving. Since 2001, InnoCentive has helped businesses harness the power of the crowd to solve problems from facilitating access to clean water at a household level to passive solar devices designed to attract & kill malaria-carrying mosquitos. Across thousands of innovation challenges, we have proven that it is not always the most 'elite' or 'educated' or even 'expert' minds in a specific field that have the capacity to solve challenges. They can be solved, anywhere, by anyone, at any time.

This book came about to pay tribute to the untold tales of unexpected people, in unlikely circumstances, solving innovation challenges from around the globe. These stories were submitted by the Solvers themselves, and are about their experiences, backgrounds, thoughts and feelings in being part of a global open innovation community with InnoCentive.

We know that innovation and ideas are everywhere. What we often underestimate is the power of many minds versus a few. Extending problems out to a wide diverse network rather than a small team of subject-matter experts – can – and indeed will (this is proven) deliver results. There is something humbling and powerful in the fact that ordinary people can contribute to extraordinary things.

This book aims to highlight this and offer insight, a new perspective, and a better understanding into the power of the crowd.

The information provided relating to specific challenges or solutions for businesses is anonymized and purposely kept vague to protect intellectual property. We believe these stories offer a unique and untold perspective and have collated them with the aim to highlight how connecting people with problems creates opportunities for new ideas to blossom and change the world.

This book is dedicated to the unsung heroes. To those problem solvers that offer their wisdom and experience to solve business challenges, not for recognition, but to explore, learn, develop and contribute to something bigger and play a role in something significant.

Diversity is central to Challenge Driven Innovation because different perspectives often approach and solve challenges in unique ways.

1.

Find your passion, then learn and discover

HISTORICAL SMART CROWD

"People who end up as 'first' don't actually set out to be first. They set out to do something they love." Condoleezza Rice

It has always been difficult to be the first to pioneer new truths in science, technology or innovation. It was particularly challenging in the past for many to be published or recognized for their work and contributions to innovation. Such things as class, gender, status, race and upbringing bore much larger weight (though many may argue they still do today).

pioneer

verb
To develop or be the first to use or apply a new method, area of knowledge, or activity.

Amateur innovators and inventors have a long history, and in today's education obsessed world it's easy to forget that some of the greatest discoveries were in fact made by amateurs. We start by paying tribute to five amateur innovators, who despite the above challenges, left a lasting legacy on the world, driven by true passion, perseverance and commitment to their fields of interest. Their discoveries have changed the world we live in.

"To reach a goal you have never before attained, you must do things you have never before done." Richard G. Scott.

HISTORICAL SMART CROWD

I am Ada Lovelace

I was a pioneer of computing

I lived in England

The world's first computer programmer

B_{50}

Ian Smyth 2020

DISCOVER MY STORY OVERLEAF

My name is Ada Lovelace - I was the world's first computer programmer, at least in the theoretical sense!

I was born in 1815 by the name Augusta Ada Byron, the only legitimate child of Annabella Milbanke and the poet Lord Byron. My mother, Lady Byron, had mathematical training (my father used to call her his 'Princess of Parallelograms') and she insisted that I study mathematics too – this was an unusual education for a woman in this era.

When I was seventeen, I met a man called Charles Babbage, a mathematician at a party and it was at this party that he demonstrated a small working section of his automatic mechanical calculator designed to tabulate polynomial functions which he named the Difference Engine. I was immediately entranced and inspired by this machine and it was this experience that fuelled my love for mathematics over the next decade. Babbage continued his research and came up with a prototype for a new version of the machine (the Analytical Engine) which would be the early makings of one of the first general-purpose computers.

Given my intense interest in Babbage's work, between 1842 and 1843 I translated an article written by Italian military engineer

Luigi Menabrea on his latest proposed version of the Analytical Engine (a programmable, general-purpose computer), supplementing the article with an elaborate set of notes. I aligned with Babbage on developing these notes, and was in regular correspondence with him over this period. The notes are around three times longer than the article itself and include in complete detail, a method for calculating a sequence of Bernoulli numbers using the Analytical Engine, which might have run correctly had it ever been built.

I considered my work to be significant in building on and extending the potential of the Analytical Engine. I believe that the machine could manipulate symbols in accordance with rules and that number could represent entities other than quantity. My research are the markings of what we now know as the first computer program – that is an algorithm designed to be carried out by a machine. I even saw a use for computer programming outside of mathematics, something visionary for the time. It's a shame though, because of the era in which I was born as well as my gender and education, my research and ideas were not taken seriously or even considered until well after my death in 1852.

I'm Ada Lovelace, I'm an amateur mathematical enthusiast, that came up with concepts and ideas in math and computer programming that changed the world.

HISTORICAL SMART CROWD

My name is Robert Evans - I am the most successful individual hunter of supernovae

I was born in 1937 in Sydney Australia and graduated from the University of Sydney, majoring in philosophy and modern history. By day, I'm a minister in the Uniting Church of Australia and, by night when the constellations are in the right position, I take my amateur 12 inch telescope out on my back porch in the Blue Mountains and hunt supernovae - dying stars.

I was introduced to the night sky by my father who had been a Scout leader and had a working knowledge of the constellations. My father could remember the botanical names of a thousand or more species of plants that grew around Sydney and the Blue Mountains, he had a detailed memory of those kinds of things, which I suppose was passed on to me. When I was about 14, my brother, an optometrist made me my first telescope out of a couple of rolls of paper and a spectacle lens. It wasn't much better than the naked eye, but it focused my interest. Then I worked at a bookshop for four years and read a book called Galactic Novae written in 1955. That book contained pretty much all the accumulated knowledge on the fifty supernovae recorded to date.

A supernova is a star that explodes, entirely or almost entirely. There are two explosion mechanisms. One of them involves a star at least five or ten times larger than the sun that runs out of nuclear fuel. The big stars burn up their juice a lot faster than the smaller ones. Once the nuclear fusion process reaches a stage where the core of the star, being made out of iron, is involved, the process is unable to continue any longer. That process is reasonably well understood by scientists nowadays—it's called a Type 2 supernova and the supernova in the Large Magellanic Cloud is one of those kind and has been studied in a lot of detail. The other process creates what are now called Type 1a supernovae and no one's ever observed one of those sorts of stars exploding, but you can get spectra of the things and usa supercomputer to create models.

One thing that astronomers have been studying for many years is the expansion of the universe. It was generally believed that the galaxies would either just continue steadily going apart or else, because of gravity, their expansion would slow and then they would start coming back together again. Supernova studies were one of the means for testing this out. About 70 percent of Type 1a supernovae are of a standard character. In the 1980s and early 1990s, a good proportion of the nearby supernovae that provided the landmark information were actually found by amateurs and a good many of them were my discoveries.

I first took up supernova hunting in 1955, and made my first official discovery in 1981, using a ten-inch Newtonian telescope which I assembled myself! When I first began observing galaxies, fewer than 60 supernovae had ever been discovered. Some of my discoveries have helped astronomers track the history of our universe. My most notable discovery was the Type 1a supernova in 1981, I then found another 14 of this type, which were fundamental to our understanding of the size of the universe and the rate at which it is expanding. I have memorized the starfield foregrounds and positions of around 1500 galaxies and at the time, could detect changes simply by looking at them through my telescope. There's something satisfying, I think, about the idea of light travelling for millions of years through space and just at the right moment as it reaches Earth someone looks at the right bit of sky and sees it. It just seems right that an event of that magnitude should be witnessed.

All told, I discovered 42 supernovae by visually viewing and memorizing 1500 galaxies and spotting when something different happened in any one of them. I also discovered a few additional supernovae with the aid of photographic comparison.

I'm sad to say that these days I have been left behind by science. Although I still hold the record for visual discoveries, I cannot compete with the technology. It's such a big industry in universities and observatories, where they have equipment that can cover the whole sky in one night. Nowadays professionals can find supernovae that I would never see in 100 years. By the time a supernova is bright enough for me to see it, they would have been able to find it a week earlier! I spent my life dedicated to searching the sky for evidence of supernovae, the massive explosions that signal the death of stars – and I don't regret a thing.

HISTORICAL SMART CROWD

I am Henrietta Swan Leavitt

I was an astronomer

I lived in the US

The woman who discovered how to measure the Universe

Ian Smyth 2020

My name is Henrietta Swan Leavitt - I am the woman who discovered how to measure the universe.

I was born in July 1868 in the town of Lancaster, Massachusetts, USA. I am the eldest of seven siblings, two of whom died at infancy. My father is a minister and worked for the church most his life. Our family was financially well off and my father's work kept our family on the move from Lancaster to Cleveland and then to Cambridge, Massachusetts, the home of Harvard University.

In these times, Harvard did not admit women, so I was enrolled into an educational establishment operated by the Society for the Collegiate Instruction for Women and graduated in 1892 age 23. My degree included math and astronomy – oh how I loved astronomy! I spent two years volunteering as a research assistant at Harvard's observatory as I worked towards a more advanced degree in the field.

In 1902 I received a permanent staff appointment hired by Edward Picking to sort, classify and study thousands of photographs of the night sky and stars taken at the observatory. Our role was to determine the brightness of all measurable stars. I believe they called us 'computers' and as women, we were generally seen as detail-oriented and suited for the often boring and rote work of data analysis. Pickering employed about

80 women at the observatory as 'computers,' paying most of us around 25 cents an hour. Although this may sound like a low wage, it was in fact higher than the average wage in America at the time, which was about $10 a week.

I excelled in this role and soon advanced to a position of head of the photographic stellar photometry department. It was here that I discovered a peculiar quality of a group of stars called ceiphids. I had by this time already devised my own system for measuring the brightness of stars and I applied these measurements to the ceiphids. In my research and sampling I discovered that some stars have a consistent brightness no matter where they are located – making it easy to figure out their distance from Earth. Instead of offering wild estimates for how far objects are from us, with my system I could measure their distances!

Although my findings were published in 1912, my work was not truly recognized until well after my death in 1921 at the age of 53. Although I was not fully appreciated as one while alive, I'm an astronomer and I made a significant impact on science. My discoveries provided astronomers with the first "standard candle" with which to measure the distance to faraway galaxies.

HISTORICAL SMART CROWD

I am Michael Faraday

I worked as a scientist

I lived in England

I solved the electromagnetism and electrochemistry challenge

My name is Michael Faraday - if at first you don't succeed, try, try, try….and try again.

I was born in South London in the late 1700s. My father was a blacksmith and my mother was a country woman. I grew up with three siblings and I had a difficult childhood. Our family was extremely poor, and we often did not get enough to eat. My father was often ill and incapable of working steadily. I recall as a child being given one loaf of bread that would need to last me the entire week.

I was not educated and learnt the basics of how to read and write at Sunday School in our church. I earned money by delivering newspapers for a local book dealer/book binder, and when I was 14 I was lucky enough to become an apprentice. While working at this store I took the opportunity to read and absorb the books that were brought in for rebinding. The article on electricity in the third edition of the Encyclopedia Britannica was particularly fascinating to me! Reading these books sparked a lifelong interest in chemistry and electricity.

My luck turned when one of the customers at the store gave me a free ticket to a lecture given by Sir Humphry Davy, a famous English chemist, at the Royal Institution. I was truly inspired and hastily wrote to Davy asking for a job as his assistant. I was turned down but in 1813 there was an opening and Davy appointed me the job of chemical assistant where I learned chemistry at the elbow of one of the greatest practitioners of all time. As my chemical capabilities increased, I was given more responsibility.

Over my life my key areas of research and discoveries were focused on electric currents, magnetic fields and mechanical motion. I was the first to produce an electric current from a magnetic field, I demonstrated the relationship between electricity and chemical bonding, I discovered the effect of magnetism on light, and I discovered and named diamagnetism, the peculiar behavior of certain substances in strong magnetic fields. However, my most notable achievement was in September 1821, when I built a device, you'll now understand to be the first electric motor. This early discovery was a major breakthrough for me, and I spent the next decade of my life trying to understand the physics behind electromagnetism.

I am nothing if not devoted to discovery through experimentation. Something to know about me, is that I never give up on ideas. When I come up with an idea, and I know it is a good one, I'll keep experimenting (no matter how many multiple failures) until I get what I expect to be true.

HISTORICAL SMART CROWD

My name is Eunice Newton Foote - I am a Climate Scientist Pioneer who connected the dots between CO2 and global warming

I was born Eunice Newton Foote in 1819 and lived most of my life in upstate New York. I was one of 11 children and with my mother was a home maker and my father was a farmer and entrepreneur. I attended Troy Female Seminary where, as students, we were encouraged to attend a nearby science-based college. It was this school that inspired me and helped me to pick up the skills needed for scientific experiments. I married my husband Elisha Foote, a Judge who was also an amateur scientist in 1841.

At home we had a lab which meant I could keep experimenting independently and over this period I became especially curious about what happened to gases when they trapped the sun's heat. I was so intrigued by this concept I wrote a paper in 1856 about my experiments, explaining that a cylinder with moist air became warmer than one with dry air. A cylinder filled with carbon dioxide warmed even more, and, once removed from the light, it took longer to cool. I discovered then that an atmosphere of that gas would give to our earth a high temperature. Little did I know at the time that I had in fact uncovered the first greenhouse gas experiment and connected the dots between carbon dioxide and global warming.

My paper was recognized at the time and presented at the annual meeting of the American Association for the Advancement of Science — but given the times, where women in science was not prevalent, it was presented by a male scientist, Joseph Henry.

It was because of these arbitrary 'societal' rules that science is not my only passion. I'm a proud and prominent feminist, suffragist and was part of many women's rights movements. I signed the declaration that emerged at the 1848 Seneca Falls Convention, one of the nation's first organized events for women's rights. My name is fifth on the list.

I was not recognized as a scientist while I was alive, but I'm proud to say I was the first person to demonstrate how different proportions of carbon dioxide in the atmosphere would change its temperature.

2.

To solve a problem, you must first understand it

Super Solver Deepak Aghor

ONE SMART CROWD

I AM DEEPAK AGHOR

I LIVE IN INDIA

I WORK AS A SCIENTIST

I AM A
SUPER SOLVER

My name is Deepak Aghor - "I believe that the solution to a problem lies in the problem itself"

I was born in a middle-income family of teachers. My family had a special regard for formal education. Because of this it did not need much convincing for me to embark on that path. Initially I wanted to do engineering but due to lack of financial support I had to opt for science. So, what was a loss of engineering was a gain for science. I initially did my B.Sc. from a regional university and became a schoolteacher for a year to save enough money so that I could further my education . I had a hard time understanding our education system, it was very broad and I thus felt the need to specialize in chemistry after considering job prospects that it offered.

I entered IIT Bombay after clearing its entrance test and enrolled for Masters of Science. Thankfully, they also awarded me sufficient financial support so that I could complete my course. This is where my real learning started. The type of education system that the institute has is both intensive and extensive and had some of the most fabulous teachers, people who really love what they do as if on a mission, and I remain grateful to all to those who largely made me who I am today. This is a place where I was introduced to research and led to two choices, to complete a PhD or to branch out into a hybrid discipline that was more tuned to the entry in the work force. I chose the latter option.

I joined IIT Delhi for a course in Analytical & Process Control techniques that looked at chemical process control. Simultaneously I completed a project in polymer science that gave me my first job, but later went back to analytical instrumentation doing various jobs in Analytical Methods Development.

I first heard about the open innovation challenges through a friend of mine who thought I would be well positioned to participate. The first challenge I came across was, I believe, about silver recovery. Later, I came to know of a chromatographic separations challenge. It was a fairly routine thing as I was a practicing chromatographer in those days. It was a two-page solution that was different from run-of-the-mill and offered another perspective while separating such molecules. It was not a particularly well written solution and I did not (at this point) understand the difference between the different types of open innovation challenges. Regardless, the company found value in what I submitted!

I don't consider solving challenges on the platform a hobby, I merely want to put my knowledge to use so that somebody benefits from it. I also learn a lot about what I don't know. I don't believe in comfort zones. If you are too comfortable then you have not tried hard enough. You can always give up after trying hard and it is not a disgrace but not trying is! Trying makes you fitter for the next challenge, it enriches you and ultimately these small imperceptible improvements start adding up one day and then you become a different person. This is what I strive for. To continuously push myself, learn and grow. Whenever you don't pass the muster, raise your standards – is a saying I live by.

I believe that the solution to a problem lies in the problem itself. I love solving challenges that are well written. In my opinion, these are the ones that bring out the best in you. One of the toughest but best challenges I worked on was one on alternative techniques for weighing small amounts of organic powders. The challenge was deceptively simple but was very clearly written, listing out all the do's and don'ts. It was fun writing the solution and even better being awarded for it! Of the total prize pool money of $30,000, a total of 12 solvers were chosen for awards. I got $18,000 while the remaining 11 solvers got $12000.

My advice for anyone thinking of participating in a crowdsourcing style platform is to simply think clearly. Try and think of it as a challenge you are facing from a personal perspective. My specific approach to problem solving is erecting a scaffolding around the problem. I decide on the vantage point that looks most promising and later-on modify the approach based on the constraints of challenge.

The idea of providing a completely open source platform to people anywhere around the world has brought substantial benefits to hundreds of thousands of people's lives. To me, it can be seen as a step in a long chain of events where even the nature of employment is set to change permanently. The open innovation model gives advantage of the 'just-in-time' and 'just-for-the situation' resource availability which I think the world is heading into more and more. It brings about enormous value through delocalization and something I appreciate from a very personal level.

ONE SMART CROWD

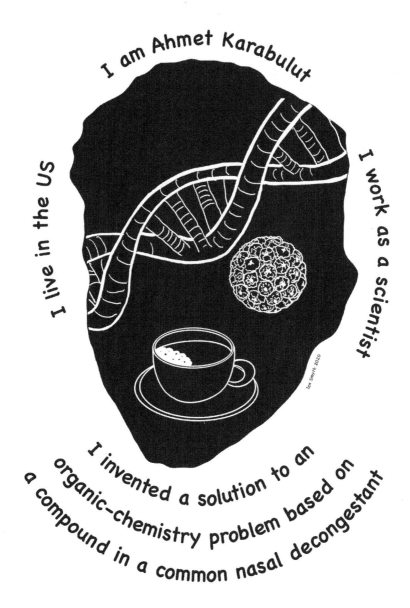

I am Ahmet Karabulut

I live in the US

I work as a scientist

I invented a solution to an organic-chemistry problem based on a compound in a common nasal decongestant

Ian Smyth 2020

My name is Ahmet Karabulut - "I was fascinated at how open innovation had emerged, evolved and became feasible enough for company R&D teams to consider the platform as a standalone part of the troubleshooting and development process for continuous innovation."

Phenylephrine is a nasal decongestant medication used for the temporary relief of stuffy nose, sinus, and ear symptoms caused by the common cold, flu, allergies, or other breathing illnesses. The medication works by decreasing swelling in the nose and ears, thereby reducing discomfort and making it easier to breathe. In the health industry, new methods to stabilize a pharmaceutical drug phenylephrine are needed.

I am a scientist, with a background in molecular biology and molecular genetics. I have been a member of the open innovation community for several years. I was recognized as a top problem solver alongside twelve other people across five countries. On joining the platform, I browsed through the various problems for a while and, out of curiosity, I submitted a couple of proposals to test myself. Several weeks later, I received serious feedback and my proposal to stabilize phenylephrine, a nasal spray component ended up being awarded $20,000.

At the time, I was fascinated at how open innovation had emerged, evolved, and became feasible enough for this company's R&D

teams to consider the platform as a standalone part of the troubleshooting and development process for continuous innovation.

After solving this first challenge, I submitted solutions for other challenges and was awarded for solving several of them. This experience has done more than earn me prizes — it has also enriched my career. Once I added these accomplishments to my resume, I started to get many more responses to job applications. I believe that the awards showed that I could troubleshoot and think creatively with originality and insight - skills that many employers value.

You could say that the solutions to the challenges I was awarded came about spontaneously, but I do not believe this happened by chance. It was only after I reviewed the problems in detail, understood them in depth, re-imagined the experimental conditions for my solution, and went through an incubation phase, did I have a solution that I believed would fulfill the requirements.

The most enjoyable part is knowing that the R&D teams of the businesses seeking these solutions were carefully evaluating proposals from anonymous submitters with as much care as the people who were participating. It was obvious that the proposals were reviewed in detail according to the quality of the ideas proposed and the suitability of the solution. The whole process was also a very convincing experience for me to realize that this double-blind process was indeed a wonderful opportunity for young scientists such as myself.

The process is managed effectively so that the best results are achieved without companies having to reveal any critical trade secrets that would otherwise be a serious issue. Fundamentally, the platform operates effectively by bringing together the world's most talented people and letting scientific experts from different research backgrounds contribute to the R&D department of the companies seeking innovative solutions. Scientists like myself can provide these solutions and recommend new ideas with creativity.

I have always been interested in scientific research and experimentation and I try to learn as much as I can from different scientific disciplines. You could say that I have an intrinsic hunger for knowledge. It is very satisfying when I get the opportunity to utilize this seemingly unconnected knowledge to address a scientific question, which is one of the benefits I get receive from being part of a community of innovators and problem solvers.

I credit my success in life to my parents who always stimulated my intellectual curiosity. My father worked in a marine biology lab and my mother was a teacher. They encouraged me to leave my home in Tarsus, Turkey, to attend university and further my education and to always be curious.

ONE SMART CROWD

I am Aaron Renn

I work as an urban analyst

I live in the US

I solved the increasing public transport use challenge

My name is Aaron Renn - "Professionally, I've worked mostly in the technology space, but I also developed an interest in urban affairs, including transportation, economic development, branding, the arts, and architecture and design."

The Chicagoland area is the third largest city ranked by population density in the United States and has the second largest public transportation system in the country. Such a high density population significantly impacts the environment both locally and globally. Electricity, natural gas, and transportation are the main sources of Chicago's global warming impact. 91% of Chicago's emissions come from these three sectors—therefore emission reductions must come from these areas. Without mitigation, Chicago's emissions of 12 tons of carbon dioxide equivalent per capita in 2000 is expected to grow 35% by 2050. The Chicago Transit authorities are searching for strategies to increasing public transportation ridership up to one billion rides per year, a feat that has not been met since 1948, to significantly reduce the emission caused by automobiles on the roads.

I grew up in a small town in rural Indiana. Although I loved the countryside, after graduating from Indiana University with a business degree, work carried me off to Chicago where I fell in love with city living. Professionally, I have worked mostly in the technology space, but I also developed an interest in urban affairs, including transportation, economic development, branding, the arts, and architecture and design. A couple of years ago I started writing my own blog on these issues, though I have long been a writer on the subject. I also published a very early internet blog about transit in Chicago in the 1990's.

One of the people who reads my blog notified me about the Chicago transportation challenge, saying it looked like something I would be interested in. Indeed, I was, and felt I had a lot to contribute to the cause of boosting public transit ridership in Chicago. Chicago is notorious for its traffic problems with bottlenecks and gridlocks as daily occurrences experienced by many drivers. To get the city moving they need to get people out of their cars and using mass transit.

The twin fold aims of this particular problem was to come up with ideas of how to increase mass transit use to 1 billion rides per year while simultaneously reducing the greenhouse gas emissions from cars. More than 125 proposals were sent in from all over the world including some from Australia, Kenya, and Japan.

In constructing my solution, I placed priority on vastly improving the experience of riding transit. I believe the values of mass transit are in conflict because of disagreements over the role of transit today and the absence of a game plan for what it should be in the future. Transit is seen as a public service, a social service for the poor and the disabled, a solution to traffic congestion and pollution and a tool to revitalize urban neighborhoods. Programs today that may provide some boost to ridership - free rides to seniors or using transit to link the inner-city transit-dependent with suburban jobs - do so at the cost of creating a societal view of transit as primarily a social service. To achieve significant market penetration, transit needs to be seen as a public service.

More than 125 thinkers from around the world proposed their ideas alongside my own, on how to increase regional mass transit ridership and reduce the environmental impact of greenhouse gas emissions released by heavy traffic. My 18-page proposal detailed precisely how the Chicago Transit Authority (CTA) can reach that billion riders mark.

One of the key components to my submission was on variable pricing. I suggested that the CTA should charge higher fares during peak travel periods. This would encourage many commuters to adjust their schedules and travel during less excessive and less costly times, easing the strain on rush-hour buses and trains. I recommended a rise in overnight track work. 'L' trains can move at a snail's pace because of workers on the rails. Repair on these trains should be moved to the hours when it will affect the fewest riders. I advised a change to 10-car trains because a few simple platform expansions could result in a 25% increase in capacity on the Blue Line. Rather than extend the Yellow Line, the CTA should consider building stations on the route that already exists such as stations at Ridge, Asbury, Dodge, and Oakton. I strongly advocated free transfers because I believe riders should not be forced to pay to switch between lines or modes of transport. The current concept means that riders pay a penalty for not having a direct route available. This is backwards. If it were feasible to do so, it should actually cost less if you have to transfer to make up for the inconvenience! I also advised on the implementation of bus-only lanes. Although is an idea that the CTA has already considered experimenting with, it was another step in my overall plan.

I love Chicago, and my motivation for submitting my proposal was to help make it an even greater city than it already is.

ONE SMART CROWD

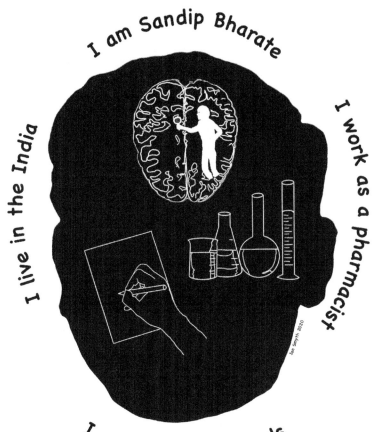

I am Sandip Bharate

I work as a pharmacist

I live in the India

I contributed towards improved drug development for Lupus, a deadly auto immune disease

Ian Smyth, 2020

My name is Sandip Bharate - "Working as a Solver is an opportunity to help change the future of innovation, and in turn create more opportunities for ourselves."

In the past 40 years, there have been very few therapeutics approved for Lupus, an autoimmune disease characterized by acute and chronic inflammation of various tissues of the body. The lack of effective and safe drugs against Lupus has taken a toll on the lives of patients with this disease, both in terms of morbidity and mortality. On average, it takes nearly six years for people with Lupus to be diagnosed, from the time they first notice their Lupus symptoms. Ninety percent of people living with Lupus are women and most people develop the disease between the ages of 15-44. Lupus is two to three times more prevalent among women of color.

There are many challenges to reaching a Lupus diagnosis and it's known as "the great imitator" because its symptoms mimic many other illnesses. Lupus symptoms can be unclear, can come and go, and can change. A comprehensive review of the history of Lupus drug development along with actionable recommendations on how this process could be improved is needed.

I am a workaholic. I love working in the lab, writing research papers, and staying in touch with recent happenings in new drug discovery. I am a passionate researcher for drug discovery & development. It was during my undergraduate course in pharmacy when I developed a keen interest in the field of medicinal chemistry, and I have constantly nurtured it during my Master's and PhD programs and professional experience.

I have been actively involved in medicinal chemistry research in the last 20 years. This is an interdisciplinary research area incorporating synthetic organic chemistry, biochemistry, pharmacology, molecular biology, and pharmaceutical chemistry in the search for better drugs. In fact, as the discipline has grown, it has embraced several other disciplines and is constantly evolving and rapidly expanding its domain.

My curiosity and interest in drug discovery led me to actively participate and win a challenge on Lupus drug development, even though I knew very little about the Lupus disease. The problem attracted me because of its clear and specific project criteria. I was very excited to learn in detail about the deadly autoimmune disease and further understand the hurdles involved in discovering new drugs for its treatment. I spent a couple of weekends trying to understand the reasons why there were a large number of failures and only few successes in Lupus clinical trials. Writing a proposal for my submission was difficult but I found it interesting and a valuable learning experience.

I submitted several successful proposals within one year and was recognized as one of the top problem solvers of the year in 2009 within the Solver community. I am proud to be a part of this fraternity where research holds an important key in fulfilling the needs of the society and in helping people live healthier lives. This business model is a very innovative way for companies and scientists and ideas to come together. I liked the concept and was excited to submit a solution to test my competence, demonstrate my capability, work my brain without limitations and compete with others to find the best solution. It was also a great chance for me to win a monetary reward.

Initially I was not clear about this unique platform. I registered quickly, but it was only after two years of regularly visiting the website that I made my first submission. From there, I then went on to win three awards in a single year and gained recognition as one of the top problem solvers in that year.

The platform helps industries solve problems, opening issues up to the whole world and thereby making a brain-storming exercise for researchers to think about these problems in a novel way. Since the community is highly competitive, there is always a risk involved in solving challenges. For me it's great to exercise the brain and a good reason to learn more about a particular research area. It's an opportunity to help change the future of innovation, and in turn create more opportunities for ourselves. I am happy to be a part of this community and look forward to solving more challenges in future. Though I am not finding much time now to work on problems, but I am definitely looking forward to getting into this again.

ONE SMART CROWD

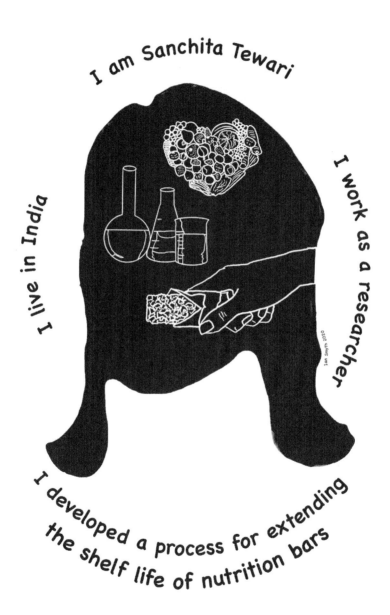

I am Sanchita Tewari

I work as a researcher

I live in India

I developed a process for extending the shelf life of nutrition bars

Ian Smyth 2020

My name is Sanchita Tewari - "Become a winning Solver marked a significant step in my professional career and an important event of my life. This was the first time I received recognition and reward from an international authority and it was a life changing experience for me and my family."

Driven by the increasingly busy lifestyles of consumers, grab-and-go convenience is experiencing rising demand among consumers. Nutritional bars have the tendency to harden over time and this makes the bar more difficult to eat. Along with hardening, the bar can also become more brittle or chewy, leading to increased chewing time and "tooth packing" – undesirable attributes for the consumer. The high demand for nutritional bars has boosted the market and there is stiff competition among manufacturers to continually introduce new products with added benefits. A typical nutrition bar will harden during its shelf life, though a fully coated bar seems to fair better over time. A manufacturer was searching for ideas to extend the shelf life of their nutritional bars to at least 18 months through the addition of a new ingredient or modification to the bar production process.

Become a winning Solver marked a significant step in my professional career and an important event of my life. This was the first time I received recognition and reward from an international authority and it was a life changing experience for me and my family. It helped a lot in my career advancement. I was truly honored to receive my reward; it is an incredible achievement for me.

I heard about the platform through one of my colleagues and one of the key reasons for joining the community was to be recognized in society for problem solving. I think that some part of me also craved the fame that comes with being a solver and I cannot deny that financial rewards is a good incentive!

The problem that I solved was about the preventing nutrition bars from going hard and coming up with a hardness removal procedure. I would love for my solution to be used in industries for developing useful products in the future.

Facing real life challenges and problems of companies across different industries is the draw for me. When technology is so advanced and knowledge is so readily accessible, as a Solver you have nothing to lose and everything to gain from this process. I think my background and domain knowledge in chemistry, life sciences and food sciences help me to problem solve across a relatively broad scope.

In my spare time I like to read scientific literature and apply some established solutions or proofs to various problems. My key piece of advice to people hoping to win a challenge is to spend a significant amount of time understanding the question and then proceed to look for the answer or feasible technology available.

ONE SMART CROWD

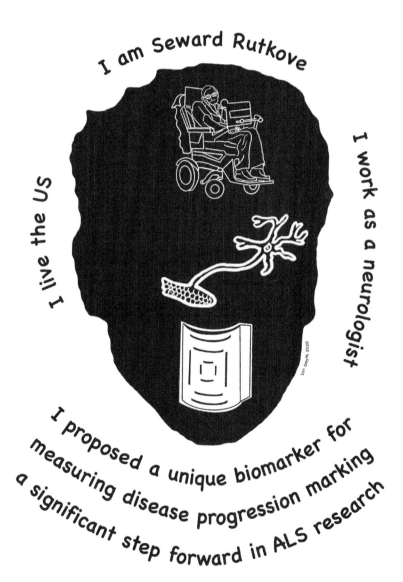

I am Seward Rutkove

I work as a neurologist

I live the US

I proposed a unique biomarker for measuring disease progression marking a significant step forward in ALS research

Ian Smyth 2020

My name is Seward Rutkove - "This challenge helped push me to improve upon our methods of data collection and to make our first handheld prototype device a reality"

Amyotrophic Lateral Sclerosis (ALS or Lou Gehrig's Disease) is a fatal neurodegenerative disease in which a person's brain loses connection with the muscles. ALS is usually characterized by selective death of motor neurons in the brain and spinal cord. This leads to muscle weakness, atrophy, and gradual paralysis. People with ALS slowly lose their ability to walk, talk, eat and eventually breathe. The disease typically strikes in people aged between 40-70 and over 5000 people are diagnosed with the disease each year. At present, there is no effective cure or therapy for ALS and patients usually die within 2-5 years after the onset of symptoms. ALS is often diagnosed by ruling out other diseases, which can take many months or even years. To accelerate the identification of effective treatments for ALS, a biomarker (an early read of disease progression) for measuring disease progression is needed.

I am a neurologist in Boston, having graduated from Cornell University and Columbia University's College of Physicians and Surgeons. I completed my neurology training at the Harvard-Longwood Neurology Program and a fellowship in clinical neurophysiology and neuromuscular disease.

I have focused my career on taking care of people with neuromuscular disorders. This includes people with relatively mild problems such as carpal tunnel syndrome, to people with more severe diseases, such as muscular dystrophy and amyotrophic lateral sclerosis (ALS).

Early on, I learned of the limitations of the current diagnostic modalities for these conditions and became determined to improve them. For this reason, I have worked to develop and refine the technique of electrical impedance myography (EIM). This technique offers the possibility of evaluating muscle painlessly and non-invasively. The research on EIM has been funded through multiple sources including the National Institutes of Health, the Amyotrophic Lateral Sclerosis Association, and the Spinal Muscular Atrophy Foundation.

I was already in the process of collecting data on ALS patients when I learned of the ALS challenge posted. It led me to apply my technology research specifically to ALS, focusing on both the animal studies and device development. It helped push me to improve upon our methods of data collection and to make our first handheld prototype device to sensitively measure disease progression a reality. EIM can measure the flow of a small electrical current through muscle tissue. The current travels differently through healthy and diseased tissue, and by evaluating the characteristics of the electrical current, EIM can accurately measure the progression of ALS disease. I continue to explore and refine EIM techniques and their interpretation in the hope that they may one day be applied widely to help evaluate and treat anyone with a nerve or muscle disorder.

The challenge offered widespread visibility of me and my team's work and research. Although we did get funding from different foundations to support our research, without this challenge, there's a good chance that even years after publishing our first paper on this technology, we would still be on the outside looking in.

ONE SMART CROWD

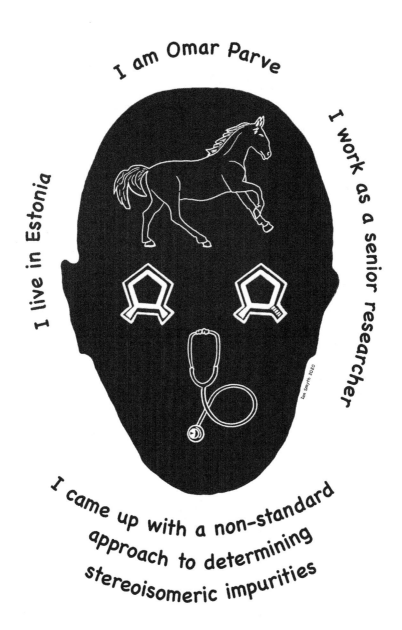

My name is Omar Parve - "To my surprise, I was the first researcher from Estonia to have won a challenge and by now, I have passed on the word about the challenges to my younger colleagues."

In absence of defined standards, the Seeker is looking for new methods for determining the stereoisomeric impurities of a pharmaceutically important target material.

Methods for the determining the stereoisomeric impurities of a pharmaceutically important target material in the absence of standards is desired. While current analytical techniques are available for determining purity with respect to non-isomers, the ability of current technology falls short in determining isomeric purity in the absence of authentic standards of the possible isomers.

The company is searching for a non-standard approach for determining whether or not there are diastereomers, especially if the endo-ester diastereomer is present in the shown olefin target material. Most importantly, a method is sought which gives one confidence in concluding that an isomer is NOT present in the olefin target material at levels as low as 0.1%.

My parents were veterinarians. My mother served as a chief veterinarian of a county. I spent the first ten years of my life in a veterinary hospital because the family of the chief veterinarian was given lodging in a villa on the territory of the veterinary hospital. I participated everywhere and in everything, and "knew exactly" what kind of medicine had to be injected to a sick horse, cow or dog. I was allowed to watch all the operations that took place and observed how my parents and other experts were discussing diagnosis and making decisions about treatments. My father had a PhD degree in his veterinary field related to horses and also had strong academic interests. He was always writing in the evenings and on weekends while I was growing up. He has written handbooks, several articles and chapters in university textbooks.

These experiences I had in my childhood are an important driving force behind my research interests which include: medicinal chemistry, drug development and synthesis of active ingredients of medicines of very high stereochemical purity. I have always had a preference for challenge-based innovation, contributing to highest-quality solutions to practical problems.

I remember having somewhat unexpectedly found a challenge bulletin in my mailbox. It was interesting reading material and I highly appreciated the free access to detailed problems that needed solving. Finally, a challenge on stereochemical problems caught my eye – it felt like a personal challenge. The details were attractive because of its clear, direct and honest style. I felt that due to my long-term experience in the field I could offer something of value to the business and the people working on finding a solution to this problem. Therefore, I proposed my (awarded!) solution.

I find this platform inspiring for its multidisciplinary aspect. It offers information about important problems in my own field of research as well as related fields. I feel I have received a lot of useful information and have now given something back by solving a real world problem. I am certainly interested in participating again to deliver more innovative solutions in the future. Having been very active in sports in my youth (competing in light athletics locally and playing basketball), one of the motivating factors in participating in a competition – like this platform - is the pure thrill of it, the joy of the 'game' so to say. Perhaps it's also out of curiosity to measure our own thoughts and research results against a global scientific community.

To my surprise, I was the first researcher from Estonia to have won a challenge and by now, I have passed on the word about the challenges to my younger colleagues. The possibility of contributing to help other people in their work, in order for them to provide a solution quicker, is definitely always a strong motivating factor behind a decision to submit a solution.

Getting to the point of providing a competitive solution is a road that in natural sciences often involves a group of people. You very rarely go at it alone. I have been lucky enough to work in a globally competitive research environment for a long period of time. It has been enjoyable, supportive and I have been imbued with trust as a researcher and always open for novel ideas.

A small anecdote from the 90s to illustrate this: we (a professor, PhD student and I) had to monitor nuclear magnetic resonance (NMR), a novel biocatalytic process for 24 hours in a row. And then, just after midnight, the director of the institute, Professor Endel Lippmaa who had been informed about our experiment, suddenly appeared in the laboratory. He came to see us just out of sincere interest in how we were getting on. At that time this professor was a highly esteemed academic as well as a political leader of Estonian society. He had vast experience and had initiated NMR studies in Tallinn, Estonia in the late fifties of the last century. His laboratories were among the leading NMR centers in Europe for decades. I admit that the traditions, experience and high level research in analytical chemistry carried out in professor Lippmaa's institute (currently the National Institute of Chemical Physics and Biophysics) enabled me to propose a winning solution in the field for the challenge that I was awarded.

3.

Thinking about many problems can help you solve one

Super Solver Yury Bodrov

ONE SMART CROWD

I AM YURY BODROV

I LIVE IN RUSSIA

I WORK IN RESEARCH

I AM A
SUPER SOLVER

My name is Yury Bodrov - "My most inspired challenge was participating in the NASA Challenge. All of us dream of space in our childhood and for many, I'm sure, this dream remains when we become adults."

I was born and now live in St. Petersburg, Russia. I'm married and I have two daughters 17 and 10 years old. I have been interested in chemistry since childhood. My mother was a chemist and she instilled in me a keen interest in chemistry. My mother, my grandmother and my grandmother's sister were heavily involved in my upbringing and education. They tried to pass on all the traditions of our family to me. Therefore, it is to them that I owe of all my future successes.

In high school I engaged in science via a research laboratory for school children and conducted research in the field of plant growth stimulants, thin layer chromatography and in the field of biologically active substances. At university, I studied the chemistry and technology of biologically active substances. I was planning a scientific career and enrolled in postgraduate studies. However, that was the time when the Soviet Union collapsed and the entire system of science in the USSR disintegrated. I was forced to leave postgraduate studies due to financial difficulties, to survive and earn money. I was in business for a while, then worked as an engineer and scientific consultant for various commercial chemical companies. This allowed me to master many new directions and become expert in the fields of chemical engineering, forest chemistry, petro chemistry and in many interdisciplinary fields.

Regardless of this experience I always wanted to do scientific research. As my scientific career was broken because of the prevailing external circumstances, I felt a significant unrealized potential in myself. Currently, I am interested in an interdisciplinary field at the intersection of nanotechnology, quantum biology, biophysics, neural networks, quantum computers and artificial intelligence. In particular, I have an idea on how to build a fundamentally new artificial intelligence system based on an innovative element created on the basis of hybrid nanostructures. My dream is to get access to a well-equipped laboratory and a good grant to implement all my ideas.

Since I have always liked to solve non-standard scientific and technical problems and I began to search for information about the existence of such problems on the Internet. It was absolutely by chance I came across crowdsourcing and discovered the opportunity to solve complex scientific and technical problems for reward. Without question, I immediately decided to participate. On the one hand, I could use my unrealized scientific potential, and on the other hand, I could make money for my family with my own mind! But it turned out that not everything is so simple. I registered on the website and started submitting my solutions for published scientific problems but all my solutions kept getting rejected!

Now, having won many challenges, I understand that my first solutions were a fiasco, primarily because they were absolutely badly framed. It's so important to properly format solutions, and I was lucky enough to receive support and a kind of template for submitting solutions that I have been using for many years now. But even having learned how to correctly formulate and present my solutions, I won my first challenge five years after I started participating in challenges.

The first challenge I ever won was about coming up with an additive to the Chlorinated Polyvinyl Chloride polymer (CPVC), which in the event of a fire would prevent the combustion of this material. I suggested a smart additive that, in the event of a fire, activates and fights the fire. My solution was accepted, and I received my first award. It was a fantastic feeling! I was incredibly happy, and it helped me believe in myself. This first success kept my enthusiasm high and gave me strength to participate in other challenges.

My favorite challenge was the Open Philanthropy Project Challenge: Bioinspiration and Unusual Biology. The main task of this challenge was to describe a biological process or material that is unusual in some way that may or may not be well understood. I was interested in this challenge because in the sphere of my scientific interests there are hybrid nanostructures and functional devices and materials based on them. I had several ideas for the solution that proposed the use of bioinspiration in the development of chemical/biological sensors for various applications. In my opinion, this solution completely met the project criteria because the phenomenon of biological receptors is not fully understood and their mechanism of action is not completely clear. Unfortunately, my solution was rejected. Despite this, it's my favorite because I get real pleasure from scientific creativity that these types of challenges provide. It gives me the opportunity to realize myself not only as a solver, but as a scientist also.

My most inspired challenge was participating in the NASA Challenge. All of us dream of space in our childhood and for many, I'm sure, this dream remains when we become adults. When I received the good news that my solution for the challenge on Keeping Food Fresh in Space won, I was extremely happy about that. I just imagined that my idea, albeit in an adapted form, could be implemented in a real NASA Mars mission. This is a great honor and it is a chance to possibly touch a lifelong dream.

One of the most surprising challenges for me was the Heart Implantation of a Medical Device challenge where I needed to propose a method of temporarily implanting a medical device inside the chamber of the human heart's ventricle. I am not an expert in the field of medicine, but I immediately had an idea how to do this. For me, working on this project as a whole was truly way out of my comfort zone, because in order to describe the solution, you need to understand the structure of the human heart and the vessels that surround it, as well as how it functions. I had to first read many chapters from an anatomy textbook on this issue, as well as scientific articles on Percutaneous Intervention to truly understand it before working on my submission. For the solution itself, I used an analogy from physics and parallels with my experiments, which I conducted in my school physics laboratory so many years ago. In this case the combination of my newly acquired experience with my past experience allowed me to solve this challenge and I was awarded a partial reward!

Perhaps nowadays, solving challenges is more of a career than a hobby, since my main motivation to participate is my lack of fulfillment in the scientific field. If I had built a scientific career, had a professor position at the university, then I would not have taken such an active part in solving scientific and technical problems on the platform. I simply would not have enough time and energy for this, since I would be spending all my potential for scientific creativity on conducting my scientific research in my lab, and I would receive all the bonuses due to my rating in the scientific community based on the results published in scientific journals. But because I do not have this, I continue to participate and will do so in the future and the winnings keep my enthusiasm alive.

I do not use any specific approach in my submissions. I just offer a solution, I try to describe it in as much detail as possible. The solution either comes immediately, or there is none at all. And in my experience, trying to synthesize solution through painful deliberation is less effective than the solution that immediately pops into my head. Sometimes I feel like I've offered the perfect solution, but it is rejected as a result and other times I think my solution is weak, but I am awarded. Why? I think it depends on many factors. I have had feedback which they said that my solution was too complicated or too expensive, therefore, even if your solution is perfect, it is not always correct and this should not upset you. I think the main advice is to turn off emotions. In general, you shouldn't care whether your solution will be accepted or rejected, because you should understand that it is absolutely useless to hope that your solution will be accepted unconditionally. Just treat it like an adventure and have fun with the creative process.

The most important advice I would like to give is that you should always go your own way. This is what will make your solutions unique. Namely, the uniqueness and variety of solutions are expected by the companies posting on the platform. Therefore, we, Solvers, must be completely different with unique backgrounds, mentality, education and thinking.

ONE SMART CROWD

I am Agung Nuswantoro

I work as an inventor

I live in Indonesia

I solved the humanitarian air drop challenge

Ian Smyth 2020

My name is Agung Nuswantoro - "What's unique is that the "AHA" moment comes while thinking about several Challenges simultaneously."

Over 2 million tons of aid has been delivered by airdrops over the past 20 years to areas cut off by emergencies, according to the World Food Program. In theory, airdrops are one of the most effective ways to get humanitarian supplies into a disaster situation, however in practice, air drops can be costly, ineffective, and often dangerous. Humanitarian food and water drops are usually the last resort for aid delivery as they require staff on the ground to create visible and unpopulated drop zones because there is danger of falling debris to people below. An air force research lab is searching for new and innovative ways to drop large quantities of food and water packages from an aircraft without injuring anyone on the ground.

I was born in Malang, Indonesia. Being an inventor has always been my passion, although the profession is not well recognized in my country. Most people become flustered if you say you are an inventor. Since my childhood, I've been very interested in science and technology. I don't know why, but I find serenity in scientific things. As I grew up, my interests spread to many fields including design, military, sports, psychology, sociology and politics.

I like being creative and seeing the world with a different perspective. I often question how things, people, or situations might appear or function from a different perspective. I also love reading and sketching; some of my other hobbies include disassembling things and then reassembling them or creating something new out of the parts.

I graduated with a degree in mechanical engineering, with a major in energy conversion. I worked for several years in R&D for an electronic manufacturing company. However, I found my job was only dealing with people, paper, and bureaucracy - no research and design as I had wanted it to be. Therefore, I resigned, and I currently work as an independent inventor.

I discovered the platform while searching for design and innovation contests, a habit since I was in high school. I've always enjoyed participating in design and innovation competitions. Although I don't always receive an award, the experiences have always enhanced my knowledge and skills. To me, these open innovation challenges posted are different in many ways. It's not about winning or losing - it's about people pushing their limits and solving others' problems, even without knowing each other.

My solution for the humanitarian air drop problem came from the coal industry and used some aspects of a fire extinguisher system. Having an interest in military technology helped me a lot when developing the solution. I got my winning idea just about 10 days before the deadline, after trying several different designs over many sleepless nights. I came up with a powered conveyer system where different food or water items could have separate timed releases based on real-time data about windspeed, terrain and drop locations up to the point of drop to prevent dangerous mishaps.

Most of the problems posted are definitely not simple; some are very exhaustive to think about. But solving problems is fun, it makes me learn new things and fuels my mind with creativity. What's unique is that the "Aha!" moment comes while thinking about several different problems simultaneously. Though it's not guaranteed that I will find a solution, thinking about solutions is incredibly exciting.

ONE SMART CROWD

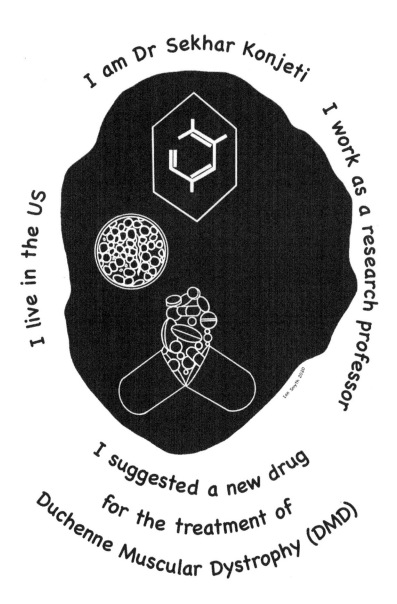

I am Dr Sekhar Konjeti

I work as a research professor

I live in the US

I suggested a new drug for the treatment of Duchenne Muscular Dystrophy (DMD)

My name is Dr Sekhar Konjeti - "My curiosity in drug discovery led me to actively participate in my next challenge even though I knew nothing about Duchenne Muscular Dystrophy (DMD)."

Duchenne muscular dystrophy (DMD) is a genetic disorder that causes muscle weakness and wasting that primarily affects young boys before the age of 5. Children born with DMD have a fault, known as a mutation, on their dystrophin gene. Dystrophin is found in all muscles in our bodies and plays an important role in protecting our muscles while they are working. The dystrophin gene is only located on X chromosomes and since boys only have one X chromosome, DMD is much more common amongst boys. DMD is classified as a rare disease since there are only ~300,000 cases worldwide. Recent advances in research are aiding the increase in life expectancy of DMD patients. The challenge posted asked to identify a drug candidate from FDA approved drug list for rapid approval for DMD.

I was trained in chemistry and obtained my PhD in organic and medicinal chemistry. I'm a Research Professor at Vanderbilt University working on drug development for cancer. I have over 25 years of research experience in biology, molecular biology and cell signaling.

I joined the open innovation community in the earlier years of its establishment. I was skeptical at first about the concept as I was concerned that I might lose intellectual property rights if I disclosed my ideas for a problem that was not chosen for the winning solution (which I subsequently learned, I do not). Despite this initial uncertainty, I submitted a solution for a theoretical problem on biological targets for inflammation. This problem required me to identify five new biological targets for the discovery and development of pharmaceuticals to treat inflammation. Instead of proposing five targets, I wrote only three targets. To my surprise, two of the targets I proposed were selected for an award.

My curiosity in drug discovery led me to actively participate in my next challenge even though I knew nothing about Duchenne Muscular Dystrophy (DMD). After reading the strategies and descriptions of the treatments, I immediately knew the solution but confirmed it by conducting a literature survey. I was concerned that it was not a drug that is approved by FDA or in clinical trials. I was confident that the over the counter drug, Resveratrol, would help patients with DMD and believe it would be a better substitute for the DMD patients who were already consuming scores of pills every day. Resveratrol acts as antioxidant and anti-inflammatory drug. Recent studies have shown that it induced dystrophin levels in mice which is essential for muscle function in these patients. Thus, it will reduce the number of pills an individual with DMD has to take if proven effective in animal and human testing.

I thought at the time, that if it works, it could be easily administered without much hassle or need FDA approval. I couldn't believe it when my proposal was selected, and the company started testing the drug on mice. It gives me pleasure to know that recent scientific literature further confirmed the usefulness of Resveratrol as a drug for DMD. This is one of my favorite solutions due to its implications for future treatment for those that suffer from DMD. This will reduce the number of pills an individual has to take if proven effective in animal and human testing. In fact, recent studies in mice have proven its effectiveness. I have also provided a winning solution for a large-scale drug screening method for DMD which has been used successfully to identify several novel drug candidates for DMD.

It is exciting for me to see the different problems the industry is facing in one place. Several of the problems the drug discovery industry facing may seem simple, but after looking at the description you soon realize how big the problems really are. Many of the industrial problems are never seen or heard outside of the industry. This type of open innovation is helping the drug discovery industry by grouping scientists and researchers with different backgrounds and posting problems from various disciplines in one place.

ONE SMART CROWD

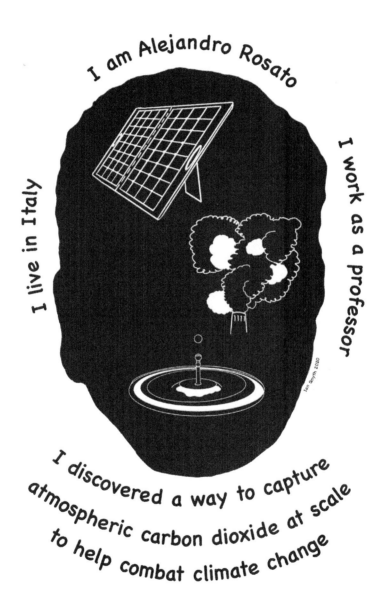

I am Alejandro Rosato

I work as a professor

I live in Italy

I discovered a way to capture atmospheric carbon dioxide at scale to help combat climate change

Ian Smyth 2020

My name is Mario Alejandro Rosato - "Your ideas are worth what they represent and contain, regardless of where you obtained your diploma or your nationality or ethnic origins."

The threat of climate change is a defining global issue. Our atmosphere is getting hotter, more turbulent, and more unpredictable because of global warming caused by the heat-trapping greenhouse gases within the upper layers of our atmosphere. With each increase of carbon, methane, or other greenhouse gas levels in the atmosphere, our local weather and global climate is further agitated, heated, and being boiled. The concentration of the human-caused carbon pollution of our atmosphere has nearly doubled in 60 years, and it is continuing to escalate at faster and faster rates. The need for a scalable and economic way to capture and fix carbon could help to address and combat climate change.

I was born in La Plata, Argentina in 1961, to a family of Italian nationals. I speak Spanish, Italian, English, French, German and Portuguese. I obtained a scholarship on renewable energy in Italy and went on to graduate in electronic and environmental engineering. Just a year later, I became a Professor of Renewable Energies. My thesis on wind turbine design was published as a book in Spain, sponsored by the European Community.

I relocated to Italy and worked for several companies, sometimes in business areas that had nothing to do with my professional background. Research on renewable energies was the first love of my life and, you know, one always remembers their first love. Since I was a child, I have always loved conducting experiments. My father was a researcher himself and introduced me to professor Elias Rosenfeld, who was a pioneer of bioclimatic architecture and renewable energies in Argentina in those days. Under his teaching, I built my first thermal solar panel at the age of 16. On my own, I built my first anaerobic digester at 17 and as undergraduate assistant collaborated with several department chairs, building a strong background in thermodynamics, thermal and electric machines, industrial economy and organization and metrology.

I founded my own business Sustainable Technologies SL, headquartered in Barcelona, Spain, and later moved to Fossalta di Portogruaro, Italy, where I run my own research laboratory. It was while working here that I discovered this platform where global problems needed solving.

It took me a few minutes to draft the conceptual idea for solving the Capture of Atmospheric Carbon to Address Global Warming challenge, and two weeks for checking calculations to ensure it would work and finally putting together all the information in a coherent document. The solution was based on some material I had translated from German into Italian for my wife's degree thesis, and from prior research I had carried out for developing a low-cost wastewater treatment system.

I have been awarded this and six other prizes so far. The second was for Rain Harvesting in Kerala. My current (2020) rating is 7 awards out of 35 solutions submitted, in a tough competitive environment. Quite stimulating, don´t you think? The thing I like about this model compared to other similar competitions of ideas is that the anonymous proposal system ensures full meritocracy. Your ideas are worth what they represent and contain, regardless of where you obtained your diploma and regardless of your nationality or ethnic origins. Also, for companies, the system allows consistent savings in R&D costs and ensures "out of the box" thinking, finally independent from the "academic endogamy" of many organizations.

When I'm not working, I spend my time visiting museums and watching documentaries. I love to research subjects that aren't directly related to my professional capacity. I have around 1.5 ton worth of books at home, mostly on science, engineering and some classic literature.

"Seven prizes out of thirty five proposals submitted, in a tough competitive environment. Quite stimulating, don't you think?"

ONE SMART CROWD

I am Sumit Bhardwaj

I work in digital marketing

I live in the UK

I came up with an efficient solution to track shipments of used electronic waste to reduce improper disposal

Ian Smyth 2020

My name is Sumit Bhardwaj - "I strongly believe that everyday people can collaborate and create simple, easily implementable, cost effective, and scalable solutions."

Electronic waste (e-waste) has been identified as one of the major roadblocks to a more sustainable electronics industry. The 50 million tons of e-waste generated every year will more than double to 110 million tons by 2050, making it the fastest growing waste stream in the world. It is too difficult to measure the true destination of e-waste such as computers, electronic equipment, devices, mobile phones and televisions etc, as they pass through the hands of downstream contractors who handle disposal and recycling.

My day-to-day job is to handle the digital marketing for a large telecommunications company in London. My evenings, weekends and other free time is spent either writing papers for my Ph.D. or working on finding solutions to intriguing problems. As someone who holds two postgraduate degrees and is currently pursuing a Ph.D. at the University of London, I am passionate about solving complex problems using technology. I strongly believe that everyday people can collaborate and create simple, easily implementable, cost effective, and scalable solutions.

The business was first described to me as "a global network to find solutions to the world's problems." It sounded intriguing enough, so I researched it a bit and signed up immediately. In an age where the extent of people's interaction on social networks can be limited to liking a post or tweeting, there are business models like this one that connect people to real-world challenges.

Furthermore, it gives them an opportunity to harness their critical thinking and contribute to something meaningful.

I started participating actively and came across the problem which sought a scalable system to track electronic waste. Considering that there are about 500,000 tons of electronic waste in the U.S. alone, it's clearly a huge problem. Moreover, sustainability is considered a megatrend. The challenge seemed both relevant and well timed, so I decided to participate and contribute what I could.

Having worked on RFID technology extensively as part of a previous research project some time back, I had a good idea of the technology's capabilities. Hence, I decided to apply the same technology to find a solution for the problem at hand. I researched some of the most prevalent ways to destroy and track electronic waste. I then researched to understand the limitations of each method, and finally chose one. The solution I came up with was to use a unique 12-digit code printed directly onto each subsystem component using a passive radio-frequency identification (RFID) link to track and measure waste from disposal to the end destination. I also studied some of the latest tracking technologies and evaluated the possibility of integrating them into my solution. The other factor I kept in mind was to ensure that the solution was economical so that it could be easy to implement and highly scalable. I submitted my solution and I was thrilled to be rewarded as one of the winning solutions.

I also participated in a challenge which sought ideas for achieving transparency in government. I suggested a Facebook app that would collect data directly from citizens, enabling government to collaborate directly with citizens and attain creative solutions to various civil problems. My solution made it to the final screening, but it was ultimately won by someone else. On reading the winning solution I really liked the other solvers' way of approaching the problem.

"In an age where the extent of people's interaction on social networks can be limited to liking a post or tweeting, there are business models like this one that connect people to real-world challenges. Furthermore, it gives them an opportunity to harness their critical thinking and contribute to something meaningful."

ONE SMART CROWD

I am Ivan Skachko

I work as a physicist

I live in Russia

I introduced a junction point in a cylindrical shaft without decreasing ultrasonic wave transmission

My name is Ivan Skachko - "I think that it is not a specific expertise that is crucial for solving problems but a special connection that is created between solver and the challenge."

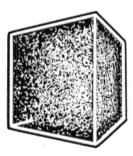

A company is hoping to find a way to introduce a junction point in a cylindrical shaft. The challenge they faced was that the shaft must transmit sound waves and the junction must be able to be open and closed. The challenge they faced was that the junction, when closed, was still a barrier to efficient conduction. Ideally the joint would conduct ultrasound energy as if it were a solid piece of material.

Starting from high school I faced the dilemma of whether to become an engineer or a physicist. I chose the latter because it seemed to be essential to get a good understanding of physical laws for either path. Eventually I understood that my true passion is designing and building things as well as solving engineering challenges. While these inclinations were of some value in my career as an experimental condensed matter physicist, I was never able to apply them to a full extent. The difficulty I faced when trying to switch to something more applied, is that the employers were usually seeking a set of specific relevant skills. My assumption that with a solid background in physics I could do anything - seemed to be disproved.

Ideation is what I often tend to do. I like to search through problems and come up with ideas that could solve them. This was the case with the challenge I was awarded. Although I had no direct experience with ultrasonic waves, the wave phenomena are very similar whether they are electromagnetic waves or sound. I was majoring in optics as an undergraduate and I was using radio frequencies in my PhD work. I also have an interest in mechanical engineering and enjoy working in the machine shop, repairing my car or doing computer-aided designs (CAD). I had some base knowledge about the topic but I learned a great deal about ultrasound while working on my submission.

I think that it is not a specific expertise that is crucial for solving problems but a special connection that is created between the person invested and problem itself. I am eagerly anticipating working on another challenge and fine tuning my ideation process!

4.

Diversity is essential to problem solving

Super Solver Ed Melcarek

ONE SMART CROWD

I am Ed Melcarek

I live in Canada

I work as a full time solver

I AM A
SUPER SOLVER

My name is Ed Melcarek - "It dawned on me that these types of problems can be solved only if you have "too diverse a set of skills and experience". Something that the corporate world frowns upon."

From a "Jack to a King", a true story. After years of being a company man and team player, I found myself trying to rescue my floundering career after being given my walking papers. My resume didn't open the doors it used to, and nobody wanted my skills as a design engineer in the local marketplace. The usual reason given by prospective employers for not hiring me was "having a too diverse a set of skills and experience" or, "are not a good fit for our needs".

If I were to hire someone to be a design engineer, I would regard any extra pertinent knowledge the applicant has, a positive attribute. But that's just me. After many years, I found that there aren't many people like me doing the hiring out there in the real world. In fact, I found that during the course of an interview, a trivial matter such as the color of one's shirt or tie can influence whether or not you get the job. An interviewer always had a hidden agenda and criteria by which the final decision was made. My qualifications, most often, had little to do with that decision. After giving up jumping through many interviewer's hoops, I decided to strike out on my own to survive in the jungle.

Burning my engineering reference library, throwing away my address book, changing my name, and getting a face lift all crossed my mind, until I came across this crowdsourcing platform. Here was a list of engineering and scientific problems asking for solutions by companies for cash rewards. After a detailed review and scrutiny, I concluded that this was in fact legitimate and worthy of my time.

Plus, something that had become just as important to me in my experience searching for a job, this had nothing to do with politics, just science. This business model also confirmed my long-standing notion of the trend in the corporate R&D world. It dawned on me that these types of problems can be solved only if you have "too diverse a set of skills and experience". Something that the corporate world frowns upon. After all, thinking "out of the box" is not something one is paid to do in the corporate world. I had little to lose with my finances down to my last dollar.

I posted a solution and subsequently won my first challenge. I came up with a method of removing dissolved impurities in dry cleaning fluid without using heat. By generating a vacuum in the containment vessel, the solvents' boiling point was lowered to a point where it could be distilled at room temperature comprising of a containment cover integrated with a vacuum pump. This cover was fitted over a standard 50-gallon steel drum with an adequate seal. The prize money saved me from the welfare office and re-affirmed confidence in myself.

My batteries were re-charged. From that point in time onwards, I went on to win 12 more awards and I am always searching and writing solutions. I've gotten to a point now where I have invested in design and modeling software and have become somewhat financially independent.

I have solved 13 challenges so far. I've given up trying to fit round pegs into square holes and jumping through the corporate status quo hoops. The open innovation business model lets me just focus on applying what I know for dollars. A dream job, considering that I get to pick and choose what I want to work on.

ONE SMART CROWD

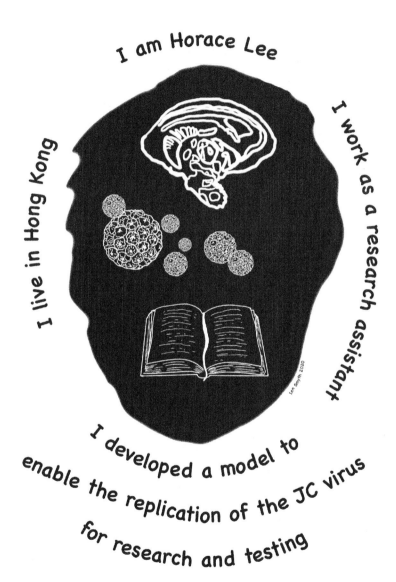

I am Horace Lee

I work as a research assistant

I live in Hong Kong

I developed a model to enable the replication of the JC virus for research and testing

Ian Smyth 2020

My name is Horace Lee - "As an unestablished young scientist born and living in Hong Kong, I find InnoCentive a vibrant playground regardless of age, education and geographical location."

Progressive Multifocal Leukoencephalopathy (PML) is a severe and currently untreatable neurodegenerative disease characterized by progressive damage or inflammation of the brain. PML has a mortality rate of 30–50% in the first few months, and those who survive can be left with varying degrees of neurological disabilities.

PML is directly associated with the JC Virus or John Cunningham virus, a common germ in the United States. More than half of all adults have been exposed to it. It doesn't cause problems for most people, but it can be dangerous if you have a weak immune system. The JC virus does not replicate in animal tissues. Strategies to make new animal models (non-human species used in medical research to mimic aspects of a disease) that would allow growth of JC virus, or a similar virus, in a non-human host are needed.

An informative animal model of this disease would allow the screening of therapeutic strategies and test the effect of drug candidates on the virus, thus allowing a kind of risk assessment for PML.

I was born in Hong Kong and went to local school. When I was working on my open innovation submission, I was a research assistant in the University of Hong Kong and HKU-Pasteur Research Centre. After that, I graduated with a PhD degree in the field of public health, virology, and immunology technology and my thesis was on animal neurodevelopment. I am now working as a post-doctoral fellow in the Department of Pathology, University of Hong Kong. I have a broad interest in science, no matter if it is related to my current work or not. Reading books and journals is my favorite pastime simply because I love science.

I have always had a passion for innovation, especially with approaches that unravel the basic mechanisms of life. However, as a research assistant I had little opportunity to innovate. When I came across this open innovation concept, I was overwhelmed with joy to discover something I had been looking for all along.

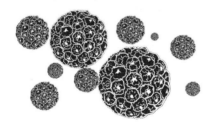

The JC virus or Polyomavirus animal model problem was a lucrative and challenging project that immediately caught my eye. I decided to give it a try without hesitation. In the first few days of my involvement, I underwent a brand-new experience since I knew nothing about the virus before. Moreover, without any experience working with mouse infection models, I had to dig heavily into the literature and started with the basics. To my amazement, I won the first challenge that I attempted. Not only did I receive a decent reward, but I was excited to see the knowledge I acquired during the innovation process to be put into practice.

As an unestablished young scientist born and living in Hong Kong, I find this concept a vibrant playground regardless of age, education, and geographical location. Anyone can prove their ability once he or she has got a good idea.

Since winning my award, I've had a son and a daughter. They are the new challenges for me. JC virus challenge is still the only challenge I submitted, I hope given my growth of knowledge and experience, I can submit another one soon.

"Moreover, without any experience working with mouse infection models, I had to dig heavily into the literature and started with the basics."

ONE SMART CROWD

I am Mike Cirella

I live in the Us

I work as an associate

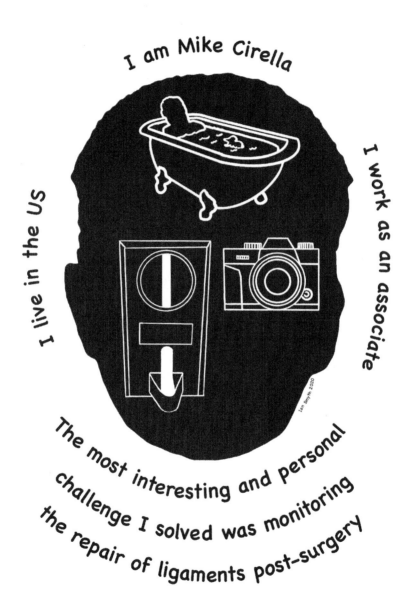

The most interesting and personal challenge I solved was monitoring the repair of ligaments post-surgery

My name is Mike Cirella - "Looking back on the challenges I have solved, the common thread that links my winning solutions is the "eureka moment" I experience after reading the description the first time and relate it to a past experience and solution to a problem in an entirely different field."

Anterior Cruciate Ligament (ACL) surgery is a common sports medicine procedure in the United States, with over 100,000 surgeries performed each year. Many injuries to a ligament or tendon require surgery to repair the damage. There are currently no relevant methods to monitor critical indicators of the healing process for each surgery. A medical company is searching for a clinically feasible micro-sensor device that could be implanted during the repair surgery to monitor displacement and mechanical load in the healing soft tissue.

Open innovation provides an opportunity to apply diverse experiences that often lead to solutions that were never considered before. So often, the 'dumb' questions are not asked by individuals studying problems from the perspective of someone inside an organization. The power of open innovation is much like a brainstorming session, where no question or suggested solution is off limits, thereby opening up the possibilities for a truly creative, and possibly unique, solution.

It is precisely for these reasons that I am an active problem solver on the platform. I have submitted many more proposed solutions than I have won, but each effort leads me down a new path and expands my knowledge for the next challenge. The process allows me to ask "why not" instead of "why," or worse, not ask at all since it is so far outside the normal approach.

Looking back on the challenges I have solved, the common thread that links my winning solutions is the "eureka moment" I experience after reading the description the first time and relate it to a past experience and solution to a problem in an entirely different field. Of course, many hours of research, organizing and fine-tuning my submission follows that moment, but the creative idea is formed by thinking laterally; searching my experience database for a tool or method that can be applied to a problem in a completely different area.

Some of my winning solutions

The off-grid task light challenge searched for a low cost, reliable charging device for home lighting in remote third world locations. where family income is low, and where there is a need for lighting that is inexpensive to buy with little or no operating costs. This problem triggered my memory of how modern coin acceptors in vending machines function reliably in harsh environments by eliminating moving parts that wear and corrode. Since the task light required a rugged, off-grid method for re-charging its batteries, I applied wind and water power, converted to electricity via permanent magnets spinning past induction coils embedded in a plastic housing.

The next challenge I solved was for an organization looking for a low cost, high speed manufacturing method to make a through-hole structure in a polymer film. The through-holes needed to be clear with hole density as high as possible while still maintaining the mechanical stability of a free-standing film. This problem had an obvious solution to me. At one point in my career, I was involved with manufacturing polarized sunglasses using plastic web handling, coating, laminating, slitting, and molding equipment. I applied my knowledge of web rollers and controls to create a simple, inexpensive solution. This was another classic example of practical knowledge of the methods in one industry being applied to a problem in another.

The perception of color challenge asked to identify methods and strategies to understand at what point in a product's life a color change will be noticeable by consumers and result in a product complaint. Physical appearance (color) is a critical attribute for pharmaceutical product quality. While color changes can be measured accurately and quantitatively by laboratory instruments, it is unclear how to correlate this quantitative data with an individual's subjective perception of color. I created a method for the drug manufacturer to better understand patient perception of color differences in tablets. This challenge piqued my interest because it applied my past experience with color vision, digital imaging, and photographic systems.

The most interesting challenge I solved focused on expediting medical care and advancing biomedical research – areas that affect everyone. Many injuries to a ligament or tendon require surgery to repair the damage. At the time, there were no relevant clinical methods to monitor the healing process. The company was searching for a feasible micro-sensor device that could be implanted during the repair surgery to monitor healing, displacement and mechanical load in the tissue. The impact of helping with this challenge struck close to home. The fact that I had personally experienced joint rehabilitation after torn-ACL surgery added to my perspective of the problem and understanding what was required in the rehab and healing process. Applying a technology that has its roots in the communications industry (another area from my past experiences) led to a powerful method for monitoring joint repair progress in a non-invasive fashion. I was proud to have won this challenge and contribute towards medical research in some way.

For me, the open innovation platform offers the diverse array of uniquely prepared minds an opportunity to apply knowledge in a creative way, addressing a problem through the mind of someone that would normally never be exposed to it without open innovation. My advice is take on a challenge! Who knows where it will lead.

ONE SMART CROWD

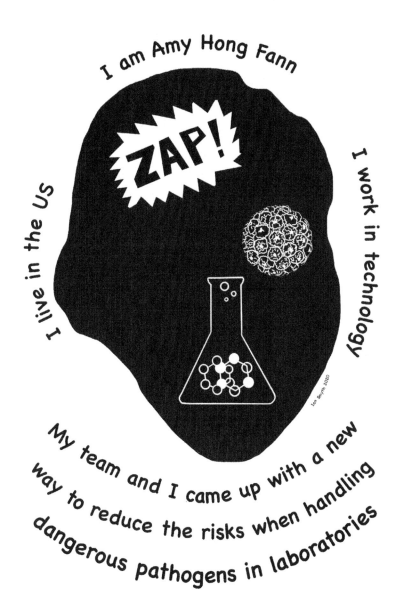

My name is Amy Hong Fann - "To be able to participate in this challenge really gave me a voice to be heard even as a layman and showed me that just because I'm not a PhD candidate, it doesn't mean that I can't contribute to the scientific community in a meaningful way.

A large number of biomedical research laboratories around the world carry out experiments with viruses that have the potential to cause significant morbidity and mortality in humans. These laboratories have equipment and procedures to minimize the associated risk but researchers still face direct risks from working with such pathogens. Furthermore, there is also a risk of either inadvertent or intentional release of these dangerous pathogens. One approach to mitigate this risk is through intrinsic biocontainment, in which a pathogen or virus is deliberately altered so that it cannot survive or spread outside of a specific environment.

I studied Molecular and Cellular Biology at UC Berkeley, with an emphasis on Cell and Development Biology: Physiology and Human Biology. I had started my undergraduate career with full intentions to become a physician, so my approach to many of my academic courses was very intellectually-oriented, where I engaged in a lot of discussion with my classmates on how to apply what we learn in real-life scenarios.

Through one of my elective courses, Introduction to Comparative Virology, I inevitably learned about viruses—how they are considered infectious agents for bacteria, plants, animals, humans —as well as the specific biomechanisms to which they can enter a cell and reproduce. The various strategies that these different families of viruses employed really intrigued me, and it made me wonder in what ways we could take advantage of their own properties for our own research benefits.

When I heard about this challenge from my course professor, I was immediately captivated and intrigued by the premise of the problem it proposed, and though my two classmates and I had very little actual expertise or knowledge in this area, we decided to take a stab and submit a proposal. We did so, not expecting anything, but approached it more as a personal challenge to try to think-out-of-the-box and come up with a solution as those who have a rather fresh perspective on the problem.

The problem was to brainstorm a novel intrinsic biocontainment method that had not been published in the scientific literature, though should be based on prior literature. The method itself should ideally be a broad strategy applicable across a range of human and nonhuman pathogenic viruses, and target viruses have the potential to pose significant danger if released without the intrinsic biocontainment method being implemented. Ideally, the method has the following characteristics: easy to use, inexpensive to use, is robust to evolutionary pressures, difficult to reverse accidentally, and difficult to reverse intentionally.

Our submission included an idea to use a novel intrinsic viral biocontainment method that can be applied to viruses in general. This method utilizes codon deoptimization in conjunction with TRNA overexpression and/or zinc-finger antiviral protein (ZAP) knockout in complementary cell lines.

Despite the little expertise we had in this field, as a group, we leveraged our teamwork and knowledge and did a lot of research by reading through scientific literature. We also consulted our professor to red team our ideas. It definitely helped to have a team who is passionate about viruses!

Since graduating from college, I had turned down an offer to medical school and decided to change careers into technology. Despite my shift in careers, I still have a lot of passion and zeal for science and biology! In the future, I would love to solve another challenge if I have the bandwidth or feel that I have something to contribute. To be able to participate in this challenge really gave me a voice to be heard even as a layman and showed me that just because I'm not a PhD candidate, it doesn't mean that I can't contribute to the scientific community in a meaningful way.

ONE SMART CROWD

I am Trevor Rose

I am setting up my own business

I live in Australia

I came up with an idea to lower the costs of banking transactions and services for the developing world

My name is Trevor Rose - "I like the idea of being an Solver because for me it's like a little billboard that will say to those who doubted me in life, that maybe they are wrong and I am a lot cleverer than I look."

Bank accounts are essential to daily economic life in developed countries but are far from universal in developing countries. According to a study in 2018, only 54% of adults in developing countries report having a bank account. The administration of bank transactions often requires the transfer and coordination of information between central offices and geographically distributed branch locations. The coordination, transmission, reconciliation, and auditing of such information represents a significant bank operating cost in the developing world. A global not-for-profit is searching to improve the efficiency of banking transactions in the developing world which would ultimately lower the costs of banking services and encourage more widespread adoption.

I have worked in over 100 jobs in my life. I've worked in various sales and customer service-related jobs, including everything from door to door sales and retail through to account and sales management, new business development and technical sales. I have done around 12 years in laboring jobs, including audio-visual work for entertainment and events, plus staging, rigging, and scaffolding, and these latter skills were also used in construction demolition and industrial maintenance. I've done everything from lifting sheep and picking fruit, through to factory work, business consulting, kitchen handing, street sweeping, car detailing, pumping gas, minding cats and houses, gardening, medical reception, and probably a bunch of other stuff that I've forgotten over the years. I can't think of a line that says "I am this", because I have done a million and one tiny little jobs, none of which were really a career in the way most people experience (meaning the money was absolute rubbish).

It is only in the last decade that I decided to become truly impoverished by becoming a mature age student, attending university to study engineering & computer science, running up a massive bill with the government. Unfortunately, I couldn't afford to finish, and the university in question wasn't turning out to be quite the value for money I'd hoped, so I decided to go back to the workforce. The reality is, I had no option but to go back to the workforce, which seemed strange as this was simultaneous to a million news reports about how Australia is so short of professional engineers and other technically trained people. I spent a good deal of time wondering why it never occurs to the decision makers to support people through education properly, and voilà problem solved. But then hey, what would I know?

When I came across the issue on improving banking processes in the developing world, I thought it sounded like an interesting problem, and one that didn't take specialist knowledge to figure out. I then read the further details and it got me thinking, before I knew it, there I was writing down the solution that came to mind. Okay, it took a bit of scribbling on paper & drawing diagrams & nutting things over, but that's part of the process I get hooked on and why I love to solve problems.

The thing I focused on was that the solution had to be viable...and what I mean by this is that when you have a very limited or closed system of known variables, sometimes there only is one solution that will actually be viable. This challenge was so restricted by the remoteness and limitations on access to banking, not to mention the limitations on the nature of the tiny transactions, that it seemed to me the answer was given by the problem description, because if you have lots of tiny (low value) transactions, you don't have the option of spending many resources per transaction, since each individual transaction isn't really worth anything. To me, that immediately tells you that the solution has to be a bulk transaction batch process, as there are no other low cost means of solving for that criteria. Then when you combine that with the remoteness, I think the rest just fell into place, because you also need it to be something the customers aren't going to lose or have to put too much effort into, because it isn't worth much to them either, unless it's a bulk amount of transactions. If every challenge was so limited as this, they'd all be easy to solve.

I do like the possibility that something I came up with might help someone in a country where the economy is very tough and perhaps make their lives easier in some way. I really hope so. For me, being a Solver is like a little billboard that says to those who doubted and underestimated me in life, that they are wrong and I am a lot cleverer than I look.

My next project is to get my own business going as an entrepreneur. I'm hoping that this will allow me to bring together the best minds I have met in life, who, like myself want to do some amazing things. There are some key areas that I hope to make an impact. I want to help businesses improve their systems, strategies, and sales. I also hope my business will impact company culture and improve external culture as well. Ideally, I'd like to make enough money to fund more of my own projects in the future.

"I can't think of a line that says "I am this", because I have done a million and one tiny little things.. "

ONE SMART CROWD

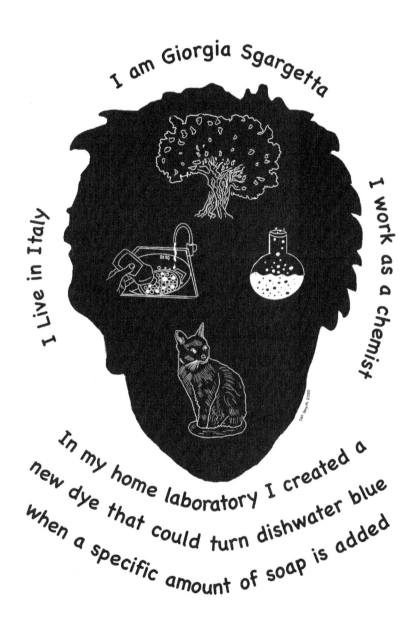

I am Giorgia Sgargetta

I Live in Italy

I work as a chemist

In my home laboratory I created a new dye that could turn dishwater blue when a specific amount of soap is added

My name is Giorgia Sgargetta - "Life to me is family and friends to trust and who trust you. My relatives and friends say that sometimes I work too hard."

The consumer goods dishwashing liquid market is highly competitive and was valued at approximately $18 billion dollars in 2019. A company is searching for a dishwashing detergent smart enough to reveal when exactly the right amount of soap had been added to a sink full of dirty dishes.

I was born in Cannara, a small town in Umbria near the center of Italy. I lived with my mom Carla, my dad Giorgio and my brother Federico. Federico is 2 years older than me and like all brothers and sisters we fought like cats and dogs growing up, although as we've grown up we are very close. I now live in Moscufo, Abruzzo (a bit further south, but still in Italy). I live with my husband, Alessandro and daughter.

After high school, I chose to study chemistry at Perugia University where I got my PhD. I discussed a thesis concerning the use of lipase enzymes in organic synthesis. My first work as a chemist was at Scala S.p.A., an Italian laundry detergent manufacturer. These years were interesting for me as I had to on occasion work on quality and assurance, R&D and I also answered the phone regarding consumer's complaints (sometimes for formulas I developed!). This experience was truly valuable to me. I then moved to Abruzzo with my family where I joined Agriformula, an Italian manufacturer of agrochemicals (but a global business). I now work in the lab and take care of safety within this environment.

I put my expertise as a chemist to work when I discovered that a consumer-goods company were searching for a dishwashing detergent smart enough to reveal when exactly the right amount of soap had been added to a sink full of dirty plates. I worked up a solution in my home laboratory and created a new dye that could turn dishwater blue when a specific amount of soap is added. Incredibly, my solution was selected as a winning solution.

Life to me is family and friends to trust and who trust you. My relatives and friends say that sometimes I work too hard. I really love to travel and I hope to travel much more in the future. My family and I live on a farm which has a lot of space for my beloved cats (number tends to increase....!). We also grow olive oil trees, 20 in total, that produce enough olive oil for the family.

ONE SMART CROWD

I am Mark Hudson

I work in product management

I live in the UK

I came up with an app idea for a cloud-based software and innovative uses of the technology

Ian Smyth 2020

My name is Mark Hudson - "My true passion has always been developing software, from very early days of developing basic games on my Commodore 64 to writing my own compiler at university."

SAP, a global cloud business software organization, sponsored a contest that challenged the developer community to create and demonstrate the most innovative use of the SAP software APIs inside of another application or process.

My true passion has always been developing software, In the very early days I used to develop basic games on my Commodore 64 and went onto writing my own compiler at university. My problem was that I was always a better software designer than developer, hence my career in Product Management rather than Product Development. After graduating from Leeds Metropolitan University (far too many years ago!) with a degree in computing and being fascinated by databases during that time, I found the application of business intelligence (BI) and data warehousing came relatively naturally and inevitably found myself falling quickly into a career focused on business intelligence.

I was lucky enough to start my career right at the beginning of the BI explosion when there was a plethora of BI vendors to choose from. Vendors which are now unfortunately only fondly remembered by employees and ex-customers.

In 1999 I realized two of my life goals, firstly to start my own business, secondly to design, develop and sell my own software. My vision was to democratize the delivery of business intelligence information to all areas of an organization. I grew the business to 15 employees, 15 blue chip customers with annual revenues of over $1m and in 2002 we were acquired.

I then set out on a new venture and became the co-founder and owner of a global business intelligence software company for over 10 years.

I still get a huge kick out of designing software with my amazing team, solving real problems faced by organizations deploying business intelligence throughout their business. The challenge that we won gave us yet another opportunity to show how we can solve these problems and was a great platform to showcase our company's innovative solutions.

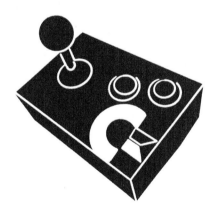

5.

You don't need to be a subject expert to solve problems

Super Solver Dmitry Tipkin

ONE SMART CROWD

I AM DIMITRY TIPKIN

I WORK AS A SCIENTIST

I LIVE IN THE US

I AM A
SUPER SOLVER

My name is Dmitry Tipkin - "My favorite challenge I worked on was for NASA concerning the radiation safety for trips to Mars. I proposed an engineering solution about a special type of magnetic field for concentration of high energy protons in special places inside the ship instead of full redirection of them."

I was born in Russia, Tver Region, in the small town of Redkino on May 21st 1968. During my school years my main subject of interest was chemistry. As a schoolboy I actively participated in so-called school scholars Olympiads and reached second place in a regional competitions. After graduating from high school, I was accepted to the Moscow Institute of Physics of Technology (sometimes called "Russian MIT") – one of the top Russian technical universities. The department was Molecular and Chemical Physics. I graduated with honors and completed a diploma specializing in electron paramagnetic resonance. I defended my PhD dissertation, devoted to applications of electron paramagnetic resonance in different areas, like mechanochemistry, conducting polymers, high-temperature superconducting ceramics.

From here I worked at various universities before returning to Russia working at the Institute of Chemical Physics and Institute of Problems of Chemical Physics in Chernogolovka. From 2006 I worked permanently in USA: first at Cornell University then at Dartmouth College. All my work was centered around free radicals and detection of them by electron paramagnetic resonance (applications and development of hardware). A few years later I found work for a US manufacturer of the detectors for high energy particles.

My comfort zone is the area of my expertise which is engineering, physics, chemistry. My more recent work in biology and medicine biomedical problems mean that these areas are now approaching into my comfort zone as well. There are challenges where new markets for existing products may be solved through preliminary analysis of the existing product. As soon as the physical and chemical characteristics are evaluated (I call my comfort zone), the new application or market may be guessed (out of my comfort zone). In a sense, even if a challenge is an the absolutely new area or topic for example pure politics, I make a start on the preliminary research of looking around the challenge to generate more information for analysis rather than looking for parallels. In the last few years (outside of the crowdsourcing platform) I've been involved in finding solutions to more complex problems in the field of "new physics" – dark matter, quantum entanglement, neutron enigma, unification of wave and particle through matter waves and some other hypothesis.

I have been an active solver for over 20 years. I've always been interested in commercialization of scientific ideas. In the early days, I thought about a database of ideas in different topics and industries being organized as an exhibition: you pay your entrance fee and then you're free to browse everything you find! So, I searched in Altavista (in a pre-Google time!) and the first result was the crowdsourcing platform. I immediately registered and started participating. This business model however was undoubtedly better than what I had in mind. I found the challenges very interesting and relatively easy to solve.

I remember the first challenge I won quite clearly. It was about new ideas for utilizing carbon dioxide solution in water and I proposed the use of silicate instead of the obvious calcium dioxide. A solution of carbon dioxide in water is a stronger acid and will drive silicon oxide out of silicate forming the complex mineral which is possible to use in bricks manufacturing.

My favorite challenge I worked on was for NASA concerning the radiation safety for trips to Mars. I proposed an engineering solution about a special type of magnetic field for concentration of high energy protons in special places inside the ship instead of full redirection of them. My solution was rejected. But what made this challenge my favorite, is that in my work at Dartmouth College somewhat correlated or could be applied to this challenge in a different way. Unfortunately, when this, completely new and unexpected solution appeared, NASA had already closed the challenge for new ways of radiation damage countermeasures.

The most unusual problem I tried to solve was the challenge where it was necessary to invent some anti-corruption scheme in science. My idea that any anti-corruption scheme in science will be the corruption scheme itself was of course rejected and I remember this challenge as an example of something unusual but also not really challenging.
A good challenge usually involves a lot of preliminary work done by the company and a clear description of previous attempts to solve their issues – this makes it really complex and challenging (the necessity to invent something new in an already crowded field). On the contrary, challenges with very broad description are not usually as interesting to me because some solution may be "googled" easily and it is sometimes not entirely clear why the business is looking for help on such a seemingly simple problem.

I once participated in a challenge as a member of the jury because they needed top Solvers to help them in identifying some of the best solutions in the early stages. I would not be able to participate in the challenge (obviously), however I instantly came up with my own solution to compare with the final results from others. I guessed one of the finalist's answers to approximately 75% accuracy - they used the same chemistry but different reagents. The other 19 finalists' submissions were completely new ideas for me. This just shows that even a top Solver by no means can predict all the ways to solve a single problem. It emphasizes important fact: it is difficult to imagine a problem, which has exactly one solution. Modern technology is so developed, usually the same problem may be solved in a multitude of ways. For an amateur solver it would be important to understand that even if your solution was undoubtedly correct, a competitor may have invented something cheaper or of higher quality.

I think that Solvers need to be patient and also be prepared for a lot of failures before any encouraging result. I was only rewarded my first prize over 10 years after submitting my first solution. The competition is enormously strong and people with good solutions are submitting their ideas from all across the globe. As far as the winning solution is concerned it is very difficult to predict it when you submit a solution. My success rate is rather low, at around 5%. I've only once been absolutely sure that my solution would win. In the rest of the cases, my wins have been unexpected – it means that it is difficult to predict what company is looking for. The situation is very familiar to start-ups. Trying to predict a product of amazing popularity is difficult, in many cases it comes unexpectedly.

For me that "aha" moment exists in many solutions but again it is not predictable! Sometimes it comes after reading the problem and sometimes after hours of checking for the necessary information. Sometimes it is absent altogether. In this case you need to calculate a solution that would work, and no instantaneous ideas lead to such solution. I would say that is the hardest type of solution to come up with - one that doesn't come to mind straight away.

I see being a Solver as more a hobby than a career despite the reward money I've won – although it does play some part I suppose! The most attractive part of working on a complex problem is the feeling of satisfaction after the solution is found. The overall experience may be compared with running a series of short sprints. It's fast work, to research, to pick up the facts, generate a hypothesis, and then develop some simple calculations to check the relevance or validity of your hypothesis. If the result is satisfactory, the feeling of deep fulfillment arises – the problem is potentially solved. I do not consider myself a "super solver" because my rate of success is relatively low. Solving problems on the platform definitely develops inventiveness. There is no doubt people who solve problems through crowdsourcing and open innovation will soon start to apply the same approach everywhere. It offers proven results! It is near impossible to publish research or results in a decent journal in the physics industry, so right now I am trying to use open innovation as a way to offer the direction for a solution to a fundamental problem in physics.

Without this experience in crowdsourcing and open innovation, I would never have even tried to work outside of my areas of expertise. My experience in working on varied challenges over a number of years now has helped me in other areas of my personal development. I now find it easier to generate ideas about "dark matter" or unification of gravity and electromagnetism, or quantum entanglement, which were previously beyond my scope.

ONE SMART CROWD

I am Madhavi Muranjan

I live in India

I work as a scientist

I came up with a model to further the research of a severe and untreatable disease

My name is Madhavi Muranjan - "There is no greater thrill in the "chase", the mystery solving and the detective work than you get out of the challenges mother nature puts out for us all, and that feeling of solving her challenges I wouldn't trade for anything else."

I came up with an animal model to further the research of a severe and untreatable disease that could have a strong preclinical and clinical impact.

An animal model is required which allows replication of JC virus. For more information, refer to a previous story on Horace Lee.

I was born and raised in India. I am creative and curious by nature and have always had a desire to alleviate human suffering caused by infectious epidemics like malaria and sleeping sickness. This is what drove me towards my Ph.D. in molecular microbiology from the Ohio State University. My passion for science was a combination of wanting to impact humanity and a strong desire to "crack the puzzle" that was my Ph.D. project. I was blessed with the mentorship of Dr. Samuel James Black, a brilliant scientist and thinker. He brought out all the creativity and imagination in me and taught me to harness it towards science.

Following post-doctorates at NYU Medical Center and Johns Hopkins, I entered the biotech industry as a senior scientist. Later as a principal scientist I was involved with both biosimilars and innovator antibodies. I learnt much about the development and the operations of science from conception to clinical trial as well as gaining regulatory approval. However, I also found that opportunities for creativity and problem solving in major corporate environments are limited.

My biotech exposure made me particularly sympathetic to patients who have suffered from PML as an adverse effect of an otherwise efficacious antibody as I worked with an antibody that had potential for this danger. For the first problem I attempted, I conceived an animal model for PML that could have a strong preclinical and clinical impact. To my surprise the idea I proposed was recognized and awarded.

It is very satisfying to study and understand new problems. But to create a possible unique solution, and to know that your idea may actually be the one to solve a major global problem - now that's really something! Besides the intense intellectual satisfaction of solving three consecutive biomedical challenges (and an additional metagenomics challenge), to me the greatest satisfaction comes from fulfilling unmet needs of humanity when any of these ideas work.

You don't have to have a strong technical background or training to solve most of the challenges. All you need to do is try your brain at something new with the zeal to learn and apply, and the awareness that it may generate intellectual property that would resolve a serious problem. Even if you don't have a complete cast-iron idea, incipient ideas flowing in the right direction can be just as valuable in the problem solving process.

For me, there is no greater thrill in the "chase", the mystery solving and the detective work than you get out of the challenges mother nature puts out for us all, and that feeling of solving her challenges I wouldn't trade for anything else.

"It is very satisfying to study and understand new problems, even more to think of a possible solution, and the best to not only get a prize in return, but to know that your idea may actually be the one to solve a major global problem."

ONE SMART CROWD

I am James Mitchell

I work as a consultant

I live in the US

I came up with a way to extract sulfur from lubricants

My name is James Mitchell - "I get a real kick out of working on a subject that is far from my inner sphere of expertise, especially when my ideas turn out to be good."

In the lubricant industry, a range of additives containing sulfur are often used as a component of lubricating oil. They are most commonly used in aerospace, automotive, military and marine services. A business is searching for unique compounds and chemistry to find and capture sulfur in lubricants to stop corrosion.

I am not a fan of research for the sake of research. I like to see a direct application of my work. I have always been interested in applying my research and reasoning skills to practical problems. It is this kind of need that fires my imagination. If there is a problem that needs to be solved, I want to contribute to the solution. This challenge model is a gift from heaven for me for these reasons!

I get a real kick out of working on a subject that is far from my inner sphere of expertise, especially when my ideas turn out to be good. Winning two awards, one on corrosion detection and the other on sulfur encapsulation for lubrication applications, are some of the achievements I am most proud of.

Sulfur is an extremely useful lubricant but is corrosive so to be used in an engine, it must be encapsulated with a high melting point inert material. These are typically metal oxides. My solution was quite complicated involving a plasma technique for metal oxide vapor production coupled with passage into a device where rapid cooling of injected sulfur vapor creates a sulfur condensation nucleus followed by metal oxide deposition onto the surface of this nucleus. Besides literature searching for thermodynamic parameters of the ingredients, this solution required a knowledge of plasma techniques, fluid mechanics, supersonic cooling techniques and cloud condensation physics. I already had experience in these areas and had been interested in encapsulation, having developed an encapsulated catalyst for smoke reduction in oil spill burning but this was produced using a much simpler method. You can imagine my delight when my solution was chosen by the client who was willing to consider such the complex process that I had proposed here.

Of course, I have submitted other solutions that were not accepted, but I did enjoy formulating them and I shall continue to send in proposed solutions in the future. What I have found is that thinking how to solve the challenges can provide inspiration for other problems that you can think of. For example, the winning corrosion detection solution that I proposed, made me think about other applications and I have used my method for detecting spilled oil on beaches as well as the detection of other substances. I even applied it to a method for detecting hidden banknotes!

In my career as a University Professor, the bulk of my research has been concerned with measuring electron-ion recombination processes which are important reactions in astrochemistry, upper atmosphere, and plasma physics. For this work I have used large particle accelerators, nuclear detection technology and ultra-high vacuum systems. Though the subject is very much an academic pursuit, I have always believed that it is important that research can have applications to larger problems. In my earlier work, I studied atomic ion recombination that is a process that prevented the temperature of previous generations of fusion machines from being increased. Only a clear understanding of this phenomenon and how to work around it allowed the present-day fusion program to progress.

I have worked on oil spill problems, seeking a method to efficiently burn oil spills while minimizing smoke emissions. This work led me to the development of a low smoke emitting fuel for firefighter training, working with scientists and oil companies in Canada and USA and with fire experts from the US Air Force. This research was really fun and involved setting fires, 100 feet in diameter, and watching them be extinguished by foam-spewing fire trucks.

I have consulted for various industries focusing on problems involving oil and gas flares, engine combustion, heat exchangers in coal furnaces, aerospace propulsion and even air conditioning. In all these diverse areas, I feel that the mental exercises that I get trying to understand atomic and molecular processes pay off in giving me an agile brain that can approach problems from a different angle and think 'outside the box'.

It delights me also to see that companies are willing to look outside their doors for ideas and to take a chance on finding answers that they might never have dreamed of.

"I have always been interested in applying my research and reasoning skills to practical problems. It is this kind of need that fires my imagination."

ONE SMART CROWD

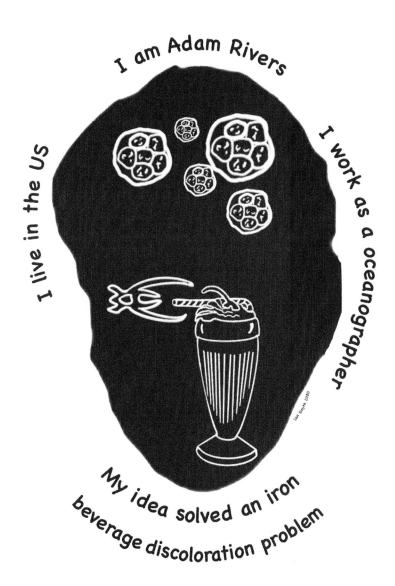

I am Adam Rivers

I work as a oceanographer

My idea solved an iron beverage discoloration problem

I live in the US

My name is Adam Rivers - "I'm always dreaming up new products or ways to improve things. If you have that kind of personality, ideas (some good, some bad) come all the time."

Flavanols are powerful antioxidants. One way in which these compounds inhibit oxidation is by complexing iron, which can generate free radicals. While this trait is desirable in the body it can produce an unappetizing food coloration by turning a purple-grey color in milk beverages. Ideas are needed to prevent unwanted food coloration in milk beverages, even when heated in high temperatures.

I recently solved a problem about milkshakes that seemingly had nothing to do with my day job working as a post doctorate in marine science at the University of Georgia. I'm a biological oceanographer by training, but the issue I solved was about iron and beverage discoloration. During my PhD, I had studied how marine microbes interact with natural iron binding chemicals called siderophores. When I read the description of the problem, I realized that it was essentially another case of an iron complexation reaction that occurs naturally in the ocean. Almost immediately, I had a few ideas. I ran through some of the kinetic equations and did a bit of kitchen chemistry, and after a long weekend, I had come up with a solution to the problem.

I keep up to date with new challenges posted. Not all of the problems catch my eye, but occasionally, there will be a problem that I quickly have an idea about. I'm the type of person that is always dreaming up new products or ways to improve things. If you have that kind of personality, ideas (some good, some bad) come all the time, but of course you can't pursue most of them. It can take years to pursue an idea academically or start a company based on an idea. The open innovation model is great because it allows anyone to invest a little bit of time writing up the sort of ideas that come to them all the time. The biggest advantage is that the problem has already been found, and my job is to focus on finding an answer. It's fun to have an outlet to apply my knowledge in unexpected ways.

I enjoy reading broadly and figuring out how to use tools from other fields. There are people who are deep subject matter experts, but that's not me. I've recently become interested with software that data mines information from social networks and want to explore what would happen if I repurposed these tools to answer questions about the ocean. I like the idea of acting as a go-between, matching a problem in one area with a solution from a wildly different realm.

I have a long-term goal to build simple devices that can describe microbial communities remotely and send that ecological information to a web browser anywhere. As a spinoff of that work, I've built a user-friendly lab freezer monitor that I'm trying to commercialize. Developing a product is a very different process; the biggest challenge is not solving a problem but making sure you are solving the right problem.

ONE SMART CROWD

I am Gregg A. Micinilio

I work as an industrial designer

I live in the US

I solved the communication platform to connect communities with climate change solutions challenge

My name is Gregg Micinilio - "I have contributed to more challenges than I have won but I always come away intellectually expanded."

Local communities across the globe need to adapt to changing climate conditions as they face rising sea levels, public health concerns, water scarcity, floods, heat waves and more extreme weather. Communities facing global warming challenges are confronted with communication gaps which often prevent connections between communities and the private sector and policy makers who can help serve and support community needs. A global non-for-profit is searching for ideas of innovative communication platforms that will help collect, aggregate, share and meet these needs and establish the tools and incentives for communities to identify, prepare and adapt to the impacts of climate change.

This problem was completely out of the realm of my area of expertise as an Industrial Designer; however, I was so intrigued by the complexity and the global need of the project that I could not walk away from it. Putting my talents to use in a humanitarian cause is an incredibly humbling and rewarding experience and I was motivated by the fact that some of my ideas could possibly, in a small way, be put to use to help a world desperate for solutions.

A well-known global environmental non-profit initiated the challenge to create a communication platform to connect vulnerable communities with businesses and governments to engage on climate change. The requirements for solutions were not limited for use in just first world communities but had to be broad enough to encompass ideas for third world countries as well. A link was required between businesses, governments, and local communities, which would create an infrastructure game plan to attack climate change issues.

As a product designer I tend to think in pictures, and as this was a written proposal, I really struggled to get all of my ideas into a coherent format. I leveraged the strength of my day-to-day job of creating communication links between different disciplines, such as marketing and engineering, and applied that to my submission. Approaching this problem as I would any other engineering or design project, I researched and gathered as much information as possible, identified the different groups of people involved, mapped a path to the most efficient and economical solutions; then I found technologies to link all the elements together. The final steps were to look beyond the obvious and to creatively expand solution directions, then figure out how I could reach desired results as inexpensively as possible, without losing value.

My solution encompassed the use of inexpensive technologies such as cell phones and cell phone apps, and free social media to simplify and track the flow of information. I also created meaningful incentives for business and academia to offer solutions beyond just feel-good humanitarian charity and introduced a more lucrative and enticing program where everyone would walk away having gained something real.

I have found that the more I branch out into areas outside of my career path, the more successful my solutions are in my own area of expertise. I truly appreciate the format of anonymous submission of proposals in the ideas are judged on their own merit - something you often don't see in the business world!

Even with just a tingle of an idea; pursue it, work it through, run it through a sieve and post it. I have submitted to many more challenges than I have won but I always come away intellectually expanded.

"I have found that the more I branch out into areas outside of my career path, the more successful my solutions are in my own area of expertise."

ONE SMART CROWD

I am Vicky Hunt

I am studying animal genetics

I live in Austria

I came up with a new marker for the treatment of a dental problem found on cats

My name is Vicky Hunt - "I am excited about my idea being put into practice, and benefiting not only the company with the problem, but also, on a practical level, veterinarians, and also cats suffering from this condition."

Biomarkers indicate the presence or extent of a biological process. Identifying biomarkers or biomarker profiles is an important step towards characterizing disease and managing disease in animals. Developments of biomarkers are linked to the ongoing clinical developments and outcomes of diseases. Feline odontoclastic resorptive lesions (FORLs) are one of the most common dental issues reported for domestic cat. A marker for Feline Odontoclastic Resorptive Lesions (FORLs) is required.

I am a student working towards a master's degree at University of Natural Resources and Applied Life Science in Vienna. I spent the previous year studying in the Netherlands. I am enrolled in a scholarship program, entitled the European Master in Animal Breeding and Genetics (EM-ABG). This Erasmus Mundus program gives international students an opportunity to obtain graduate degrees through European universities. Following the completion of my degree, I hope to work as a conservation biologist for a zoo, preferably aiding in the design and implementation of breeding programs for endangered species.

Through the Erasmus Mundus program, I have learned to appreciate the impact of cooperation between researchers with various perspectives. In my opinion, this cooperation is also an important aspect of the unique solving opportunities offered through this platform.

I received my undergraduate degree in biology from Cornell University, with a focus on animal physiology. I drew on my understanding of physiology, and on my practical knowledge of animal care and handling, to solve the challenge. I was required to describe a non-invasive marker for Feline Odontoclastic Resorptive Lesions (FORLs). Although the underlying cause is not completely understood, the risk of developing a FORL increases in older cats. These lesions are painful and lead to difficulty or refusal to eat in affected cats. Over time, there is eventual loss of the tooth crown and root; extraction of the tooth is usually necessary in more advanced stages of the disease. I am excited about my idea being put into practice, and benefiting not only businesses, but also, on a practical level, veterinarians, and cats suffering from this condition.

I am grateful to have been given the opportunity and motivation to step outside of my area of expertise and develop creative solutions for problems on a wide range of topics. I have submitted a solution for another challenge recently, and I intend to try many more in the future.

ONE SMART CROWD

I am Adrian Perez

I work in sustainable building

I live in the US

I came up with a communication platform to connect communities with climate change solutions

My name is Adrian Perez - "I find that InnoCentive reflects the spirit of the age; it takes advantage of today's connectivity, allowing for disassociated and wildly diverse input of human experience, targeting the same problem, equating to well-rounded, inclusive solutions."

Local communities are facing many global warming impacts such as rising sea levels, public health concerns, water scarcity, floods, heat waves and more extreme weather. There are several databases and initiatives with information about local impacts of climate change however, communication gaps prevent connections between communities and the private sector and policy makers who can help serve and support community needs.

A global research non-profit organization is searching for ideas for innovative communication platforms that will connect information about local community needs to public and private sector organizations who that can provide solutions, support and incentives to help community members identify, prepare for and adapt to the impacts of climate change.

I moved to Savannah, Georgia, USA from Honduras for tertiary schooling at the Savannah College of Art and Design. My academic specialty is the built environment with specific interests in systems thinking, interaction design, and sustainability. Upon completion of my schooling, I moved to Kenya where I was doing work with the United

Nation Human Settlements Programme looking into subjects such as appropriate technologies, human displacement, and climate change. I eventually returned to Savannah and became involved with an organization whose mission is to increase the value and accessibility to building material waste streams through facilitation, collaboration, education and advocacy.

I heard about the innovation platform at a lecture I attended about out-of-the-box thinking and open-mindedness. I remember making a mental note for future investigation and I have since been a loyal frequenter to the site. On one of these frequent visits I found a challenge for creating a communication platform to connect vulnerable communities to climate change solutions. The description explained that there are several databases and initiatives with information about local impacts and needs however, communication gaps prevent connections between communities and the private sector and policy makers who can help serve and support community needs. As I read through it, I became excited, as I was able to relate to certain thematic areas due to my previous experiences in Kenya. Shortly after, I began doing my research on the three main subjects of the challenge: climate change, communication platforms and human vulnerability.

Over time, I began to form parallels between the three subjects and eventually began presenting my ideas to friends over coffee. After much frustration, moments of rest and a fast-approaching deadline, a final idea was decided on and submitted. After that, I waited. I had almost lost hope of winning, when I received a congratulations email notifying me of my success and reward. I was thrilled.

I think that this business model reflects the spirit of the age; it takes advantage of today's connectivity, allowing for disassociated and wildly diverse input of human experience, targeting the same problem, equating to well-rounded, inclusive solutions.

6.

When you think you've solved the problem, push further

Super Solver Michael Kardauskas

ONE SMART CROWD

I AM MICHAEL KARDAUSKAS

I WORK IN CONSULTANCY

I LIVE IN THE US

I AM A
SUPER SOLVER

My name is Michael Kardauskas - "My mother bought us a set of children's encyclopaedias, which explained everything from photosynthesis to how the pyramids might have been built, and my father subscribed to Popular Science magazine, which touted all the latest inventions that might revolutionize the future – flying cars, etc. I devoured both of them and thought the greatest possible career would be to be an inventor."

My father was an electrical engineer, and both of my parents firmly believed that a good education was the route to success in life. My mother bought us a set of children's encyclopedias, which explained everything from photosynthesis to how the pyramids might have been built, and my father subscribed to Popular Science magazine, which touted all the latest inventions that might revolutionize the future – flying cars, etc. I devoured both of them and thought the greatest possible career would be to be an inventor. I was fascinated by inventions that would produce electricity and tried building newfangled batteries and solar cells in our basement. This was at the age of 10 or 11. By the time I was 12, I was familiar with the process of applying for a patent. By the time I was 13 or 14, I was sending suggestions for inventions to companies; one for a flashlight design that would be less bulky than then-standard designs, and one for a lightweight sleeping bag, both influenced by the camping that we were doing in the summers.

The summers were hot and the bedroom I shared with my brother took the full brunt of the sun from the south and west, so that it became quite uncomfortable. My parents bought only one small bedroom-size air conditioner for the entire house, which did nothing to cool our room at the far end of the house. My father did not want to buy another, explaining that it was a heavy, complex appliance that consumed a lot of expensive electricity. My response, at the age of 14 or 15, was to think this problem through and try to come up with a simpler device that would provide cooling at a lower cost. I concluded that a lot of the complexity of the device was due to its use of Freon, which required tight seals and a specialized compressor, and reasoned, based on my knowledge of its operating principle, that if you compressed air instead of Freon, it would still function, but it would be simpler and less expensive. I typed up my concept and sent it to the engineering department at Carrier Corporation, along with a paragraph declaring that this was confidential information, and conferred no right to use it without permission. A few weeks later, I received a reply wherein an engineer patiently explained to me that what I had invented was called the Brayton cycle, and that it is used on commercial aircraft, but it is not used in home air conditioners because it is noisier and less efficient than the conventional kind. That was a disappointment, but I was encouraged that I had been taken seriously. About one year later, I came up with an improved design for large jet aircraft, and I pursued it just as vigorously, recommending it to engineers at a major aircraft manufacturer, who wrote back to inform me that, although such aircraft did not yet exist, they had been working on that concept for about ten years. The first aircraft to incorporate the design appeared a few years later.

By the time I was in my third year of high school, I had read enough about the lives of inventors to know that they rarely earned a comfortable living, and had resigned myself to the fact that I was going to have to get a conventional job. Although I did well in my math and science studies, I knew that I did not want to be an engineer, because no matter what they may have intended to do when they started in the profession, most of them seemed to end up working in one capacity or another for the military or the defense industry. This was during the Vietnam War, and I am American, so that colored my view of the profession. I had no strong leanings toward any other profession, but I received advice (I don't recall from whom) to go into architecture, which would allow me to make use of my mathematical abilities in a creative profession, and it seemed like a logical choice. So, I entered the demanding architecture program at the University of Virginia - at the tender age of 16, because I had skipped third grade. I had no trouble being accepted into the program because I was a National Merit finalist, meaning that I had placed in the top 1% of high school students in national testing, even though I was one year younger than the others in my class year.

The decision to study architecture at UVA turned out to be a poor one. I did well in my technical courses, but did not have the outgoing personality and flair for self-promotion that were needed to stand out in the all-important design courses. I was encouraged to change majors, but instead, I dropped out of the university, and took a job in graphic arts. After four years in the graphic arts job, I recognized that there was no chance for advancement, and I was on track for being underpaid for my entire career. I perused university catalogs that I had from years earlier, looking for a program that might lead to a career something like that of an inventor. I discovered a program at Penn State University called Engineering Science that bestowed a degree in engineering, but was unconventional in that it covered not one, but all of the major branches of engineering, and was intended to produce graduates who were comfortable working at the boundaries between different disciplines, such as chemistry and electrical engineering. I was not dissuaded by the fact that this constituted the College of Engineering's honors program; of some 2,000 engineering graduates each year, only about 35 graduated in Engineering Science. Each senior in that program is required to carry out original research and write a thesis. Mine was related to photovoltaics (solar cells), which was a very active field at the time. I went on to complete my masters and then a PhD so that I would be qualified for a senior position in industry. By the time I received that degree, I was twice as old as when I entered university for the first time.

Upon graduation, I had my choice of job offers from photovoltaic companies, which were booming at that time. I joined Mobil, who were investing in innovation to make efficient solar cells from inexpensive, lower quality silicon. That task caused Mobil to pull together an A-Team of chemists, engineers, and physicists to work on this objective, and we were eventually ready to begin mass production of high-performance solar panels. However, changes in top management at Mobil Oil Corporation resulted in a shift in corporate priorities. They decided to exit the solar energy business, and sold the company to a German competitor. I went on to work for the German firm, where I acquired experience in designing and operating manufacturing equipment and processes. After several years in that position, I left to start a career as an independent materials science consultant.

Although my consulting business provided a good income, paying assignments did not always fill my work schedule. My brother, who was aware of this, came across the concept of open innovation awards and thought it would be ideal for me, providing an outlet for my creativity that could also be a profitable way to utilize free time between other, more conventional consulting assignments. I was intrigued by the concept, so I registered and set to work on my first challenge.

After two false starts, submitting solutions that were ultimately rejected, I finally succeeded in winning a challenge.

The request was for a food additive that tasted like salt, but was sodium-free. I expected this one to be easy, since I was aware that chlorides that are chemically similar to sodium chloride, such as magnesium and calcium chlorides, taste salty and are non-toxic. Unfortunately, my background research revealed that they also taste bitter. Having invested a significant amount of time, I pressed on with my search rather than giving up, intending to abandon the project if I didn't find a solution quickly. But I did find a solution, a food-safe ingredient that is even recommended by the FDA as a food additive because of its nutritional value. I received a partial award, which wasn't large, but it demonstrated that solving such challenges can be profitable. I went on to win more awards in that year and I was named a top solver in the first year that I submitted solutions. Not all of the solutions that I have submitted resulted in awards, but, over time, I became a good judge of what types of challenges I was likely to be able to solve within the required timeframe. For instance, I came to recognize that I was not likely going to be able to solve in a matter of weeks problems that had stumped industry professionals for years, and that the best challenges to work on were those with limited, clearly defined goals.

One of the challenges that was a pleasure to work on was one in which a food manufacturer who makes sugar syrup in very large quantities wanted to reduce the energy consumed in that process. Their standard method was to make a dilute sugar solution and then boil off the excess water. They did it that way because even at the boiling point of water, 100°C, the solubility of sugar is lower than the sugar concentration they needed; in order to operate at a higher temperature, they would need to run the process under significant pressure, which would require thick steel pressure vessels. I soon realized that the company was apparently unaware that the boiling point of water is not a constant, but changes depending on the concentration of substances dissolved in it. That being the case, it was likely that they could dissolve most of the sugar at a temperature below the boiling point, and that would change the boiling point, so that they could then raise the temperature above 100°C, which would allow them to dissolve more. I consulted charts and tables of the relevant data, and found that, if executed in a sufficient number of increments, this method would allow them to reach the desired sugar concentration without boiling off any water at all, reducing the process's energy consumption by an astounding 80%, and reducing process time, as well. I received a full award for my solution. It is one of my favorites because the company presented a straightforward problem, and that problem had a clear, straightforward solution, in addition to which I felt a sense of accomplishment for contributing to the elimination of so much energy waste.

More recently, I had to move my elderly parents into my home and provide them care 24/7. At first, I was still able to work on a few challenges, but as their health deteriorated, I no longer had the necessary free time, causing a gap in my submission history. Eventually, my mother passed away, followed by my father, one year later. Up to that point, by my count, I had logged into 129 challenges, submitted 78 solutions, and received 20 awards.

It has taken me a while to take care of tasks that I neglected during that time, and it was only a few months ago that I decided to work on a new challenge, one that is probably the farthest outside my comfort zone; it took me one full week just to learn the necessary vocabulary before starting my research in earnest. The challenge was to present a hypothesis as to why a medication developed and tested by a major pharmaceutical company, and approved by both U.S. and European authorities, was causing a small number of patients to lose their vision. I was attracted to this challenge by the prospect of potentially speeding up the company's search for a solution, which could prevent hundreds of people from losing their eyesight. After weeks of background research, I found that, more than 50 years ago, similar adverse events had been traced to the use of an unrelated medication; the underlying cause was so counterintuitive that it took medical researchers some 30 years to discover it. The similarity of the two cases made me suspect that a similar mechanism was at play in the case of the client's medication. I struggled to write my solution report in the style of an article in a medical journal, since I had no prior experience in pharmaceutical research. As this book goes to press, I have just received word that I will receive an award for my solution - It seems that I am back in the game!

ONE SMART CROWD

I am Jose Luis Susa Rincon

I work as a Electrical Engineer

I live in Colombia

I helped increase parental involvement in the way young people learn

Ian Smyth 2020

My name is Jose Luis Susa Rincon - "I always fancied being an inventor, because of that I chose engineering as my career: to re-invent the world. I believe in the intrinsic human capacity of innovation. We just need to believe in our ideas and believe that each new idea could make a difference. I think that anything is possible."

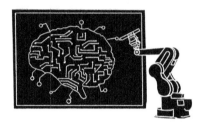

Parental engagement is a key positive driver of young people's educational achievement and fulfillment. A 2015 study showed that among parents with school-age children, 85% say they have talked to a teacher about their children's progress in school over a 12 month period. A non-profit organization is searching to find ways to improve parental involvement in young peoples learning that goes beyond traditional activities such as choosing a school, taking part in school governance, or through events such as parents' evenings.

I am now a father, a husband, a PhD. in robotics, an educator, the founder of an education non-profit in California, and still a dreamer. But back in 2011, when I solved my first challenge, I was just the latter of these things: a dreamer. With a bachelors in electronics from my home country of Colombia and coming from France after completing my master's in engineering and robotics, I felt I had all the cards in my hand to start playing in the world.

I always fancied being an inventor, because of that I chose engineering as my career: to re-invent the world. I believe in the intrinsic human capacity of innovation. We just need to believe in our ideas and believe that each new idea could make a difference. I think that anything is possible.

Neither my engineering experience nor my knowledge in robotics helped me in solving this challenge. It was my humble experience as a high school student, my will to solve problems, and my stubbornness to make things happen. However, I couldn't do it alone, so I convinced my dad to partner with me and despite our unaccountable doubts and insecurities as individuals from a developing country with no big name to support us, we succeeded.

Together, we combined our inventive attitudes, his background in psychology, his multiple years working with children and education, intelligence development, and my background in engineering to create the best team for achieving this bid.

During my high school years my father proposed a similar idea to educate parents together with their children. His unique approach to education, his past experience with coordinating a parents' school program and my memories from school shaped our solution. We iteratively improved my father's original program with a generalized method where the parents' not only took a few classes, but they also shared the feelings of being in school and understanding the importance of taking an active role in their children's educational path. I hope one day I can go and see what became of our ideas.

Winning this challenge with my father José Felix Susa gave me such confidence and opened my eyes to do more and become a full-time problem solver. I can say without a doubt that our idea is changing people's lives. It helped me to keep dreaming about impacting education and using robotics not just to help us with difficult tasks in factories or warehouses, but as a fun way to engage children into learning complex subjects like physics, math, programming, electronics and more! I like to think that we are in this world for one thing: to be happy. I try to live by this mantra and aim to live every day as the last day. As a result, I have many memorable times with my loved ones, I am happy working with my robots and education projects, but most important, it helps me wake up and smile every day.

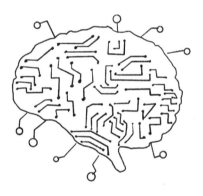

ONE SMART CROWD

I am Sheeraj Pawar

I work as a utilities consultant

I Live in India

esc.

Ian Smyth 2020

My idea aimed to solve urgent transportation problems in my hometown of Mumbai

My name is Sheeraj Pawar - "I feel incredibly lucky to have my idea acknowledged. This process has allowed me to express myself and achieve something constructive and worthwhile. It is a great boon for people who have a burning desire for the betterment of our society and have great ideas to achieve their goals."

In 2015, Mumbai recorded 23,468 traffic collisions, the highest across India. Poor road infrastructure and the lack of adherence to road rules is seen as the main causes. In 2017, an independent survey revealed that 98% of railway stations in Mumbai pose a high risk or are "dangerous" to persons with disabilities and senior citizens, lacking basic structures such as ramps and escalators. Some of the key challenges in transportation in Mumbai is the peak-hour congestion on roads, traffic collisions, public transport accessibility and increasing burden on commuter rail, with trains on average packed to 2.6 times their capacity. The challenge asks the solver community to identify an immediate problem or opportunity in your local community that needs solving.

A problem that has deeply affected my community for a long time is that of heavily strained transport management system. I will never forget how one of my colleagues slipped and lost his life while traveling on a foot board of a crowded train. This incident wouldn't have occurred if a robust transport system was in place.

In India (especially Mumbai), people are forced to travel in extremely crowded trains and buses because there are no alternative modes of transport. Due to the burgeoning population, the amount of strain is tremendous on these modes of transport. Overhauling the entire transport management system is the need of the hour.

My idea to introduce a robust water transport system and dedicated cycle lanes for commuters to reduce overcrowding and congestion was the premise of my submission to the challenge that I won. The vast coastline of Mumbai could be used for water transport and dedicated bicycle lanes (taking a leaf out of Netherlands' book) could be kept for commuters. This would significantly alleviate our existing transport management issues. This problem is being faced in many other cities across the world and I believe this idea could be scaled to other cities across the globe.

My family and friends were extremely proud of my idea and my colleagues couldn't stop raving about me. My manager also dropped an email to our entire team of 40 people recognizing my efforts. I now feel even more of a sense of responsibility to achieve the goal of making a positive impact for my community.

I feel incredibly lucky to have my idea acknowledged. This process has allowed me to express myself and achieve something constructive and worthwhile. It is a great boon for people who have a burning desire for the betterment of our society and have great ideas to achieve their goals. This experience has further strengthened my self-belief and gives me hope that I can achieve even greater goals in the future.

I am currently working with Dell Technologies as a Program Manager for Commercial and Channel Sales teams in the US and Canada. I am a recipient of the Game Changer award at Dell and also part of the top 2% cohort selected for a Leadership Program by senior leadership of my organization.

Outside my workplace, I have co-directed a short film, penned education-related articles for local newspapers and taught computer skills to children that have been abused. I am a huge soccer fan and follow almost all the European leagues! I am glad to be part of this great community where ideas are a form of currency.

ONE SMART CROWD

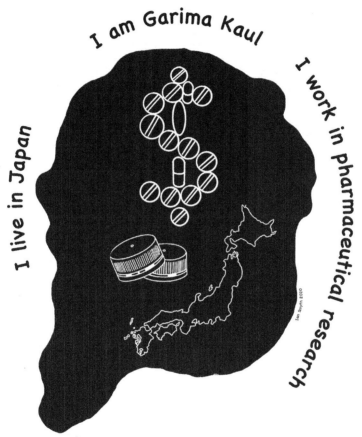

I am Garima Kaul

I work in pharmaceutical research

I live in Japan

I came up with a new way of defining 'regions' for clinical trials

My name is Garima Kaul - "Solving these problems gives me immense satisfaction and provides me with a chance to get my ideas out to the global community. This platform has not only given me an opportunity to successfully apply my skills, but it has also helped me learn."

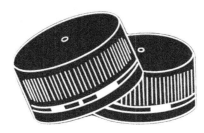

There is no standardized approach or consistent rationale for defining region when conducting regional clinical trials. To date, region is most often defined based on geography and, often an entire continent was commonly used to describe region. Given we need to have a representation of population across the globe for participants in a trial to test drugs in diverse population, is dividing population only by country the right way of selection? Ideas for new definitions of regions for clinical trials are required.

I first learned about the open innovation platform during my master's program. I continued to be interested throughout my doctorate studies in pharmaceutical technology however I could not find time to work on any submissions due to my research work. After completing my educational studies, I worked for a company in Delhi where I worked in the life sciences and healthcare division. It was only after moving to Japan and becoming a freelancer in pharmaceutical business research that I found I had the time to focus on solving challenges.

I attempted to solve problems not only related to my subject expertise but also one that I found interesting where I felt my ideas would be a good fit. Initially, when I submitted my solutions, I was never confident that I would hit the target. But after being awarded for my first solution it gave me the confidence to explore further and now each submission brings a bounty of learning and knowledge, whether I win or not. The solution came to me as a mix of secondary research and my own thoughts. Although there was time frame for submission, I only needed a week to work on it.

Solving these problems gives me immense satisfaction and provides me with a chance to get my ideas out to the global community. This platform has not only given me an opportunity to successfully apply my skills, but it has also helped me learn. I strongly believe that knowledge never goes to waste and I have become more sensitive to issues which previously did not bother me because of challenges I have read or been involved in. At times we take many things for granted or do not realize the depth of situations. Some of the issues posted, are not only interesting, but also bring to light underlying larger problems you may not have realized before.

The open innovation concept is a constructive use of working minds from all over the world. Submissions are not limited by geography, profession, or educational background, so problems are seen with different perspectives. It is an opportunity to work on realistic and complex industrial issues which they may not face personally and to look beyond their focus areas. There are no limitations or restrictions of how you approach the problem and it is totally upon your intellect and creativity to solve it.

After winning this challenge, I went on to solve more problems and was awarded three more times. This also led me to talk about the concept of open innovation in Japan, through Nature Publishing Group. More than a decade on, I still feel very highly of this business and platform. It is a great opportunity to tap into knowledge and skills from across the globe.

ONE SMART CROWD

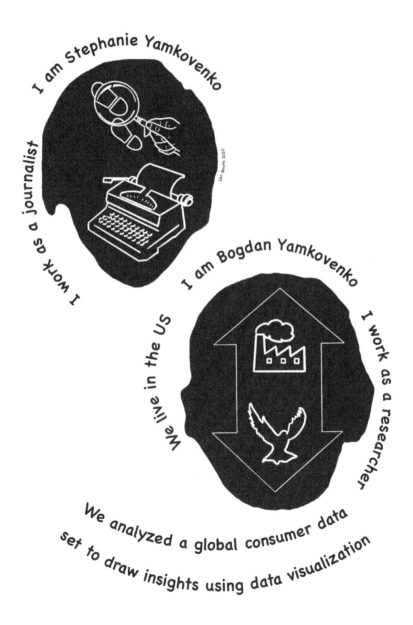

We are Bogdan and Stephanie Yamkovenko - "Bogdan and I have been married for six years and had never previously collaborated professionally on a project. This was a great opportunity for us to combine our skills."

The Economist and Neilson Data developed an open innovation challenge which asked the world to review a Nielson consumer data set to generate insightful conclusions with broad implications and present back a compelling visual presentation of the most interesting ideas from the data supplied. Over 4000 submissions were received from across 101 countries.

The focus of the challenge was to analyze a data global set and to tell a story using data visualization. The data sets of economic indicators were consumer confidence, job growth, employment and debt levels and we had to both analyze the data and illustrate the findings in graphics that could be easily understood by a broad variety of readers. I am a journalist and have also done graphic design in the past, so I knew I could handle the visual story telling. Bogdan is a researcher and assistant professor with an affinity for statistics, which means that he could easily handle the data analysis.

Bogdan and I have been married for six years and had never previously collaborated professionally on a project. This was a great opportunity for us to combine our skills and, ultimately, be competitive.

We began with a brainstorm on the dataset, which included the Consumer Confidence Index and other data about consumer spending and purchasing habits. We decided to supplement the dataset with other widely available economic indicators (such as unemployment rates). We noticed that countries that had high confidence in their economies were not necessarily the best performing economies.

When working on my master's degree in journalism, I developed an appreciation for my profession's role as the "fourth estate." As we looked at the confidence index, we noticed that countries such as Saudi Arabia and Egypt had high confidence, but their economies weren't doing that great. We wondered whether democracy was playing a role in the citizens' confidence. We decided to include the Reporters Without Borders Press Freedom Index in our analysis and found that countries with the highest confidence also had the most restricted press.

This finding gave us a compelling story to tell and gave the original dataset more context and depth. However, the Internet and social media may be game changers. As the data indicated, people want honest information. If they cannot get it from their country's press, they will turn to the internet and social media to find accurate information.

It really is a great platform for allowing individuals to work on solving problems outside of the usual confines of their jobs. Over 4000 people from 101 different countries signed up to participate – which is pretty incredible! It is also a great way to spark collaborations among people who may have never otherwise worked together on projects.

If you are working on a solution, we have two pieces of advice. Firstly, don't be afraid to do something unique, it might end up being just what the company is looking for. Secondly, I highly recommend using your past experiences and skills to your advantage. Neither of us are artists nor designers, yet we won this challenge because we found a way to solve it by playing to our strengths.

I have thought a lot about data visualization since winning the challenge, and one thing I feel strongly about is the important role it has for journalists. With every story we tell, we are using the skills necessary for data visualization: gathering information (data) from multiple sources, examining the facts, arranging it coherently, and providing readers with context and depth that will help them understand the story. That has been my key takeaway.

ONE SMART CROWD

I am Corinne Le Buhan

I work in IP and innovation

I live in Switzerland

Ian Smyth 2020

I developed a new human potential metric based on the unique "creative sharing" ability of human beings

My name is Corinne Le Buhan - "I find value in being able to connect and share knowledge from vastly different fields as my life experience and understanding develops."

The Human Development Index (HDI) is a statistic developed and compiled by the United Nations to measure various countries' levels of social and economic development. The Economist is looking for new and creative metrics or indices that draw attention to an important societal trend. Many different metrics have had profound impacts on how we measure progress and inspire people to improve the world. The challenge asks the solver community to come up with thought-out concepts for novel and useful metrics or indices to quantify important trends that affect humanity.

I'm a freelance technology consultant in intellectual property and innovation management from Lausanne, Switzerland. I wanted to better understand how innovation crowdsourcing works in practice and what new opportunities it enables for my customers. This open innovation approach was not very well known and is often feared because of the loss of control it seems to imply, but that can be addressed with the right framework and process.

I registered to test it out and ended submitting an ideation challenge on my own simply because it was inspiring to me. It's a lot of work to compile a good proposal. I had to gather the relevant information for background knowledge, and devoted further time to explore what other solutions already exist elsewhere. Next, I had to articulate my idea as clearly as possible to formalize a suitable answer based on the requirements. This process is somewhat similar to capturing a technical invention into a good patent description and claim. You need significant quiet time to think and write about it!

What particularly motivated me to devote the extra-hours building an answer was its larger purpose and meaning than what I'm usually working on. In my humble view, GDP-based metrics are depressing the whole western economies in a schizophrenic way as we grow GDP at the expense of other goals such as environmental preservation. I personally have the opportunity to interact with a number of creative and positive-minded engineers who have not given up their faith in mankind's capability to design new technologies. So, I thought there must be a way to better capture that, as a human potential index measurement, rather than with GDP-derived metrics.

These types of challenges are rewarding to work on because it is truly creative work. I find value in being able to connect and share knowledge from vastly different fields as my life experience and understanding develops and challenges like the one I submitted are a great example of this. I'm using the visibility I gained to connect to other people with the same concerns and hopes for a better human potential development measurement. I think there's room for further formalism and prototyping from real data in this area, but this requires funding. Ideas that are not implemented in the end are just ideas, not innovations…that's nice, but a bit worthless. I hope to move this to the next step and have already started to connect to others to evaluate if there's enough momentum to further build something concrete out of our respective ideas, expertise and networks.

"What particularly motivated me was its larger purpose and meaning than what I'm usually working on."

"Ideas that are not implemented in the end are just ideas, not innovations... that's nice, but a bit worthless."

ONE SMART CROWD

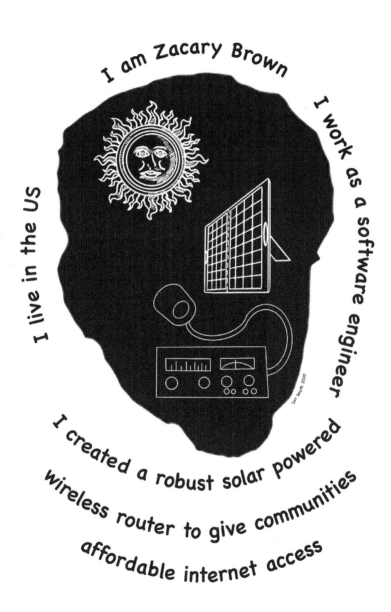

I am Zacary Brown

I work as a software engineer

I live in the US

I created a robust solar powered wireless router to give communities affordable internet access

Ian Smyth 2020

My name is Zacary Brown - "I remember my parents explaining how the solar panels that Jimmy Carter had installed at the White House could make electricity from sunlight. Both seemed like magic to me at the time."

Design a reliable solar-powered wireless router, using low cost, easily available hardware and software to provide poor communities with affordable internet access. Wireless routers are needed to connect users to an uplink. The router has to be powerful enough to cope with large amounts of data and be able to do so without being reliant on grid electricity.

I'm a 31-year-old software engineer from Texas. I have been interested in radios and solar power since I was young. I remember sitting in front of my father's antique RCA receiver as a child, listening to shortwave broadcasts from around the world as I wondered how the signals could travel such great distances. Similarly, I remember my parents explaining how the solar panels that Jimmy Carter had installed at the White House could make electricity from sunlight. Both seemed like magic to me at the time.

I studied Computer Science during college and spent a good deal of time studying the design and construction computer network protocols. I had the privilege of taking a networking course with a known professor who has been involved in network research and development since the 1970s, and who piqued my interest in wireless networking in particular.

During college, I became an amateur radio operator, and began making contact with other radio operators worldwide. My goal is to make radio contact with every country in the world. I have built and tinkered with quite a few radios, antenna systems, and ancillary components over the years. Perhaps more relevantly, I have studied the design, construction, and operation of amateur radio networks. Their purposes and components differ, but they are similar in many ways. During college, I began using the Linux operating system, which I have since employed many times in embedded systems and specialized computers such as network routers.

When I came across the wireless router challenge, I knew right away I could add value. Despite my experience I still studied the problem for a number of weeks, and the solution did not come straight away. I was actively working on it in the evenings. I got discouraged at one point but kept going and finally found the solution. I got over some of the design issues I was having by studying published papers from MIT's "Roofnet Project" which is an experimental rooftop wireless network*.

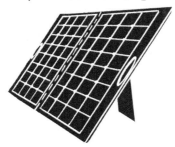

The solution I finally landed on was a Linux-based operating system that is powered by a battery which gets its energy from the sun via solar panels. The hardware is robust enough so that it can withstand outdoor use and it can be controlled remotely, so network operators are able to activate the switches with pre-paid cell phones.

More recently, I have integrated solar power into my amateur radio activities. I have constructed several solar powered stations which employ many of the same design principles that I applied to the solution I proposed in my submission. I had the benefit of already having built similar systems when I wrote the proposal and won the challenge.

A prototype of my router is being built by engineering students at the University of Arizona. I'm honored to have my solution recognized and also deemed suitable to start building – I can't wait until they progress from prototype to testing live in the field.

I found this experience an intellectual challenge, the opportunity to make a buck or two, but most importantly, the chance to make a big difference to people's lives. It is rewarding to develop something that will have such a profound impact on children in India and support a world cause.

7.

Remember, you must be able to implement your idea

Super Solver Doug Corrigan

ONE SMART CROWD

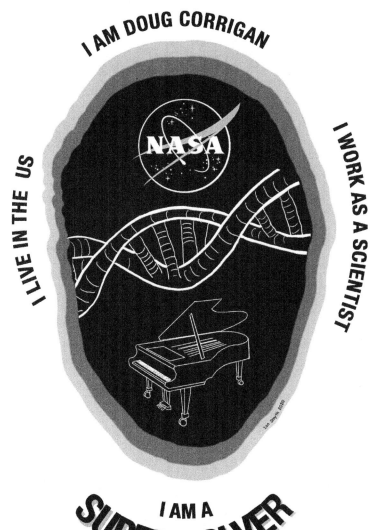

I AM DOUG CORRIGAN

I WORK AS A SCIENTIST

I LIVE IN THE US

I AM A
SUPER SOLVER

My name is Doug Corrigan - "The reason that there is a challenge in the first place is because there are already experts who have not been able to solve the challenge. If it was easily solved by subject matter experts in that field, it wouldn't have become a challenge. "

I've been interested in science since my childhood. I followed this passion as I grew older and I now have a Ph.D. in Biochemistry and Molecular Biology, a master's in Engineering, and a bachelor's in engineering physics with a concentration in electrical engineering.

As a NASA Graduate Fellow, I worked with NASA on a series of microgravity research studies that flew aboard the Space Shuttle, as well as with the Department of Energy doing research on new materials. After this, I switched into the life sciences and became involved in developing novel drug-discovery tools. From there, I became involved in the consulting industry to help bring new innovative materials and technologies to market. As a hobby, I enjoy composing piano music.

If I recall correctly, a friend had mentioned the crowdsourcing approach to me, which prompted me to look in to it more. I didn't realize this business model existed at the time, but it thoroughly intrigued my sense of creativity and desire to develop innovative solutions to difficult problems. I believe that one of the first challenges that I entered and won was based on a design for the next generation digital camera.

I thoroughly enjoy working on developing creative ideas and exercising my brain, so the challenges are a hobby that I enjoy. I love learning, and the problems always involve a substantial period of learning a new field of science or technology. Because I like learning new information, I typically have more success and enjoyment from challenges that are outside of my comfort zone or area of expertise. I also believe this initial naivety is more amenable to developing an "outside-the-box" solution. Deep domain experts in a given field have difficulty discovering innovative solutions due to ingrained presuppositions, and so someone with a "blank slate" is not restricted by those same theoretical or mental constraints. That's the beauty of open innovation whereby anyone from any discipline could be the person that solves an impossible challenge.

When submitting proposals to challenges, the key is to justify your solution. Your solution may have never been tested in real life, but you need to convince others that your solution has a real chance of working. To do this, you need to dive deep into the scientific literature and into scientific theory. For example, in the 3D glass printing example, I didn't simply claim, "print the glass from the gas phase using lasers." I literally worked out all of the gas-phase chemistry and optical physics in detail. You need to know the science in great depth, and you should be able to communicate those principles to someone who is not familiar with those concepts.

If it is a field of science or technology, you're not familiar with, you should first become familiar with this field through self-teaching. As there is a deadline to these challenges, you need to learn how to learn, fast. You will need a strong theoretical framework to build from. After you have a good mastery of the science, you should lay out the technical details of how the solution will work, and why it will work. I think many solutions fail because the Solver doesn't provide that level of theoretical framework to convince someone that the solution can be practically implemented. In all of my solutions that seemed "radical", I always provided an in-depth technical discussion that walked the reviewer through the science step-by-step. After reviewing this justification, the reviewer was hopefully convinced it would work. I strive to discover a technically justifiable pathway based on real science that proves the solution will work every time. Even if I had a potential solution, if I couldn't develop a convincing scientific theory as to how the device would work, I would abandon the concept and move on to something else.

A solution needs to be "innovative". Innovation is combining technologies and scientific principles together in a unique way that hasn't been implemented before. This is where creativity comes in. The more that you can expand your knowledge base to be cross-disciplinary, the broader your tool kit will be for pulling the necessary pieces together. I think that more creative solutions come from people who understand many different fields of science and technology. For example, the answer to a question about how to produce a laboratory model for the kidney may exist somewhere in the field of semiconductor physics. The question is then, "how well can you connect the dots from different fields?" But if you have no dots to connect, then you have nothing.

My key piece of advice is to learn everything you can, from every discipline that you can, even if it's not in your area of expertise. The reason that there is a challenge in the first place is because there are already experts who have not been able to solve the challenge. If it was easily solved by subject matter experts in that field, it wouldn't have become a challenge. Therefore, you need to get outside of your field of expertise.

An interesting challenge that comes to mind is a new type of carpet cleaner. I had absolutely no knowledge about carpet cleaners other than the fact that I despised them. However, after some research and brainstorming, I was able to develop a concept for a much more efficient and effective carpet cleaner based on design theory for rocket engine nozzles. I borrowed an innovative manufacturing concept used in the fiber-optic industry to develop a solution on how to produce a long-range nano-ordered magnetic material in high throughput over large macroscopic distances. I believe the best solutions come from completely unrelated fields.

My favorite challenges are the ones that initially seem absolutely unfeasible. If you read the initial challenge and you mumble to yourself, "good luck with that, because that's impossible!", then that's the kind of challenge I want to work on. These impossible challenges make you stretch your knowledge and question why these limitations exist. Once you isolate the barriers, you can start finding ways to circumvent those barriers. As an example, one challenge involved developing new ways of producing glass at room temperature. After I isolated the barriers, I was able to devise a solution that was based on 3D printing glass from the gas phase (instead of the liquid phase) using lasers. I think this was one of my favorite challenges to work on.

My last piece of advice is to not be afraid. If you are out of your comfort zone, this is where you will probably find the most success. Therefore, you should not be afraid to attempt solving challenges that you feel unknowledgeable about. The worst that could happen is that you learn about a new field. Remember, if the experts could solve the problem, then it wouldn't be a challenge. Your "non-expertise" is what is needed!

ONE SMART CROWD

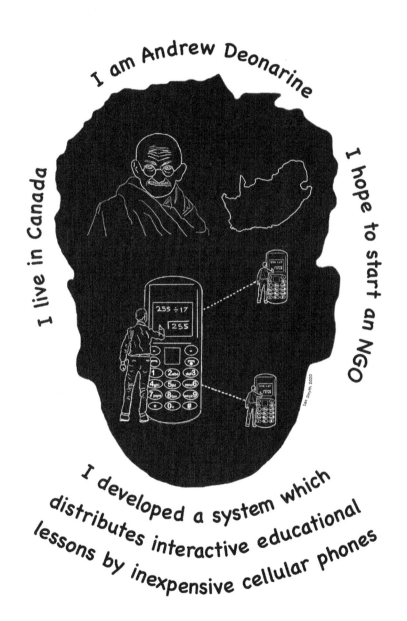

I am Andrew Deonarine

I live in Canada

I hope to start an NGO

I developed a system which distributes interactive educational lessons by inexpensive cellular phones

My name is Andrew Deonarine -
"This is something I've been working on for years. It has been amazing to get the chance to get my ideas out to the world and start to translate them from conceptual documents, emulator code, and schematics into real working pilots."

Access to education is a continuing global issue, especially for underdeveloped countries where connectivity is limited, and resources are scarce. Africa has areas with less than 50% literacy among children ages 18 and under. By comparison, the youth literacy rates in South American and European countries are among the highest with 90-100% literacy. The challenge tasked Solvers to design the model 21st century Cyber School, to address the unprecedented challenge of providing educational opportunities to the billions of school-age students in developing nations.

I'm currently a second year medical resident at University of British Columbia (UBC). I've always been interested in biology, medicine, and computer science so it seemed natural to complete my degrees and studies in these fields. I'm often asked about how my studies in bioinformatics, public health, medicine, epidemiology, and biochemistry and chemistry fit together. My answer is that I believe that one needs a holistic approach to solving developmental problems.

Often, NGOs will pursue "silo issues" rather than taking an integrated approach to development. In other words, they might look at economic development but not education, health but not economic development, or, the environment but not health for example. Some of my other interests are creating conceptual models for development and education in resource-poor areas. To address international health issues, I believe you need to have a strong understanding of technology, public health, epidemiology, education, and basic science, in addition to understanding local cultures and politics. Hence my academic journey.

I became interested in how education can be delivered via cellular phones after listening to speakers from South Africa discuss the educational hurdles faced there after the Apartheid. I've also read Gandhi's teachings on education and the importance of "universal media" in teaching. Many social, health, and economic problems in developing countries could be addressed if the populations were literate and had a basic education. In locations such as South Asia and sub-Saharan Africa, children, teens, and adults do not have access to education. Many are illiterate and cannot make use of books and other learning material. While some technologies, such as laptops and tablets have been proposed to address the educational needs of this population, the devices are too expensive, require some degree of literacy, and are difficult to implement in resource poor areas.

I developed a system called "Phonecasting" which distributes interactive educational lessons by inexpensive cellular phones, using software called "EduCell". It is a cellular phone-based educational system that has content creation, distribution, and delivery capabilities. EduCell consists of a piece of software that that runs small multi-lingual "scripts", easily developed by local teachers in developing countries. Scripts are then assembled with multimedia to create interactive modules that teach reading, writing, arithmetic, etc. Modules can then be distributed (phonecasted) to millions of other phones via an Internet server, or pre-loaded, at no cost. It provides a platform for basic literacy and can run on a variety of electronic devices, such as cellular phones, PDAs, embedded devices, and computers.

With very few maintenance requirements, EduCell can be used to educate large segments of a given population with minimal infrastructure, finances, and manpower. The benefits of the phonecasting technology are significant. Neither software programming experience nor knowledge of English is required to produce content, which democratizes software development. This would, for the first time, make basic literacy and educational material accessible to hundreds of millions of cellular phone users, and their children, around the world.

EduCell fulfills the test of being a "universal medium" as described by Gandhi, and could be an important, open-source teaching platform for the 21st century. The goal of "EduCell" is to plug the education gap that many children face in developing countries.

This is something I've been working on for years. It has been amazing to get the chance to get my ideas out to the world and start to translate them from conceptual documents, emulator code, and schematics into real working pilots. I hope to start an NGO and employ students part-time to develop this idea over the coming months, and eventually to have this technology deployed across the world. I believe that basic literacy is a pre-requisite to solving many of the world's problems, and my phonecasting ideas is the way to help the world become literate.

ONE SMART CROWD

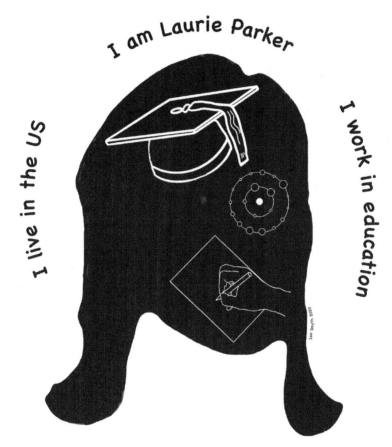

I am Laurie Parker

I work in education

I live in the US

I came up with a new approach to creating polypeptide libraries

Ian Smyth 2020

My name is Laurie Parker - "I love this site as a model for community problem solving that has options for thinkers at any level."

The problem was to develop a new approach to rapidly generate a diverse collection of polypeptide samples. This "Peptide Library" is a powerful tool for drug design, protein interactions, and other biochemical and pharmaceutical applications.

I studied chemistry at the University of St Thomas. As a student, I did not yet have years of practical experience in a lab of my own to test out new ideas. My research mentor and I did a lot of custom synthesis to supplement our research budget and were always looking for interesting synthetic problems to solve. As an undergraduate, I found that most of the solutions I came up with turned out to be the ones that were already in place, or not suitable.

A few years later I saw something that I felt I had a bit more expertise in. I was synthesizing macrocyclic polyamines at the time, and a problem was posted asking for novel methods to make a certain cyclam derivative. An issue for a lowly graduate student was reduction to practice—grad students don't exactly have the time or the resources to try the chemistry that is needed to demonstrate solutions to synthetic. Still, that became my first submitted solution, and although I didn't win, I received helpful critique and encouragement in the review of my solution. I understood that my solution was still very naïve and not efficient enough for industrial use. Plus, I hadn't been able to do any synthetic work on it, which the problem required!

As I moved into postdoctoral research at the University of Chicago and continued to develop more sophisticated skills and improve my thinking process, I started seeing more and more problems posted to which I felt I could contribute some actual expertise. However, I was still hampered by the resources problem—my responsibilities were to my grant projects and my principle investigators (PIs) who paid me, and it didn't feel right (or probably legal) to use lab resources for my own potential financial gain.

My mind was still my own though, and finally I came across a problem that was right up my alley: a paper-only request that was about the exact kind of science I have been developing for my future research. It did not require transfer of intellectual property, and they wanted some thoughtfully brainstormed ideas for different ways to think about making protein libraries. Since I already had experience in this space and had thought out a lot of the details and with the appropriate references at hand, it wasn't difficult for me to write up my new method as a solution. I was surprised and delighted to find out I was awarded for my submission. I agree that the money is great, but the real excitement is in the feeling of having contributed something useful that other people value.

I'm going to be starting a faculty position in the fall and although I don't envision myself taking the time to solve regularly, I do love his model for community problem solving that has options for thinkers at any level. Even if you don't have a lab, or are just starting out in science or engineering, it's an excellent way to hone your critical thinking and creativity and hey, you just might get lucky and have somebody need your unique expertise someday, like I did!

"As other solvers have said, the money is great, but the real excitement is in the feeling of having contributed something useful that other people value."

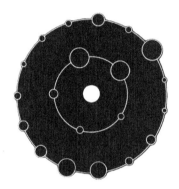

ONE SMART CROWD

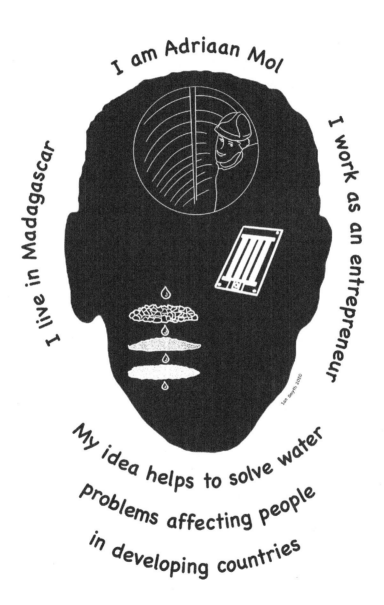

My name is Adriaan Mol - "When I discovered this problem, I couldn't resist sharing the insights and experiences I had learned. I truly hope they can be put to work and cause true change in an environment which sorely needs more attention and a lasting positive impact on the community!"

844 million people lack basic drinking water access which equates to more than 1 of every 10 people on the planet. The Seeker company is interested in ideas to address water problems in developing countries. The problem must be one that warrants a quick resolution and can be accomplished at a relatively low cost. Some key areas of interest include but are not limited to water collection, management, and efficiency.

I have worked for international relief and development organizations in Africa and Asia for over 10 years. I co-founded the social-enterprise business BushProof in 2005 as a result of growing dissatisfaction with the long-term sustainability of charitable initiatives. With few exceptions, the measurable long-term impact of donor-funded NGO projects is discouragingly low, and over time I became increasingly concerned about this.

My own 'aha' moment came a few years ago in Somalia, when I worked for a project responding to floods in the south of this law-less country. We built several community-managed village water systems that purified contaminated river water. Before construction was even finished, a conflict broke out between various clans over the ownership of the systems. Eventually, theft of taps, refusal of the community to pay for guards and unwillingness to carry out very simple maintenance ensured that all filters were out of order within months of installation.

Before construction on the village units started, I placed a simple filter made from a plastic drum near the river, to test the filter quality of locally available sand. A number of local militia men were guarding some boats, and I asked them to continuously pour water in the drum for testing purposes. Naturally, they quickly 'adopted' the filter as their own once they saw that dirty water came out clean and fresh. Not long afterwards we had to evacuate for security reasons. Frustrated by the project's failure to unite a violent and historically split community for the purpose of 'community' sand filters, I went to the river to collect the small filters. One of the guards asked me for a filter as a gift, but annoyed as I was with the whole situation, I curtly told him to pay for it or move on. To my surprise, the gunman returned within minutes with the 10 dollars I had asked him for – a substantial amount in that context. When I passed his house a few hours later, I found that his wife had established a small business selling clean water to her neighbors. Within hours several other people asked to buy small filters, but no more plastic drums were available.

This experience really opened my eyes. A gunfight breaks out in town over a free donor-funded village water system – but these same people gladly paid serious money for a privately owned solution. Thus, was born the idea of applying entrepreneurship

215

to solve some of the world's most pressing needs: access to basic social services, such as drinking water or energy, which myself and a partner eventually turned into reality. We founded a social-enterprise business, BushProof which specializes in groundwater exploitation, including water well drilling, and custom water supply technologies for remote areas and difficult environments in Africa and abroad.

The opportunity to work towards poverty reduction through a business rather than a charity is incredibly challenging but immensely motivating. Besides delivering true change, the most motivating aspect is the changed relationship with those we serve. Instead of passive beneficiaries, they are now my customers. This puts us on an equal footing, whilst forcing me to deliver true value they need most – otherwise they won't buy it. When I discovered this problem posted, I couldn't resist sharing these insights and experiences of what I had learned. I truly hope they can be put to work and cause true change in an environment which sorely needs more attention and a lasting positive impact on the community!

ONE SMART CROWD

I am Hannah Safford

I work as a researcher

I live in the US

My teammate and I came up with a method to accurately identify and quantify viruses in water

Ian Smyth 2020

My name is Hannah Safford - "I was first introduced to the concept of innovation challenges and prizes during my two-year fellowship in the White House Office of Science and Technology Policy (OSTP) under the Obama administration."

The demand for water is growing throughout the western United States. As a result, the cost of water has also significantly increased, with the average monthly bills in some cities rising by more than 100% since 2010. The country's aging and sub-standard water infrastructure is a leading factor for the increase in water and sewer bills. One of the ways the demand for water is being met is through water reuse, a method where wastewater is treated to be used again by the community. While advanced water treatment technologies exist to produce high quality, potable water from wastewater, improved virus detection and monitoring is needed to ensure treatment is always carried out safely.

My background professionally and academically has been in engineering and public policy. Both disciplines are about problem solving, though they use different "toolkits" to achieve solutions. Engineers use the tools of math and science; policymakers use the tools of economics, law, and communication. The open innovation platform concept is great for me because it's all about problem solving. But it doesn't prescribe which toolkit you use.

I was first introduced to the concept of innovation challenges and prizes during my two-year fellowship in the White House Office of Science and Technology Policy (OSTP) under the Obama administration. After I left OSTP, I started a Ph.D. program at UC Davis. This challenge came up about a year into my Ph.D. My knowledge of prize challenges and my PhD advisor's technical expertise made us a perfect team!

The problem we set about solving was to develop rapid and forward-thinking methods of detecting pathogens in water (virus, protozoa, and other disease-causing organisms). Our solution focused on how we can quickly and accurately identify and quantify viruses in water using a technique called "flow cytometry". Flow cytometry involves using a fluid like water to force a small volume of a sample into a very narrow stream. The stream is so narrow that particles in the sample have to physically line up in single file. You can then pass that narrow stream through a series of lasers. Different types of particles exhibit different light-scatter and fluorescent patterns when they pass through the lasers. By analyzing these patterns, you can quickly and accurately identify the particles that generated them.

We didn't think we were going to win this challenge when we applied since we knew the challenge was competitive and we were a pretty small problem-solving team, but we figured that you miss 100% of the shots you don't take. And this shot went in! I'm especially glad for the opportunity our win gave us to showcase the unique perspectives that my advisor and I bring to environmental engineering. We're both fairly young women—I'm in my 20s and my advisor is in her 30s—and both of us are deeply interested in policy as well as science. These characteristics allow us to bring a fresh perspective to STEM. We don't want to do science just like science has already been done before...we want to think about the intersections of STEM with education, policy, innovation, and inclusion.

The ethos of the challenge itself was a good fit for how we approach science generally. In science, success is measured by how many papers you put out, how many classes you teach, and how many lectures you deliver, which are all measures of output but not necessarily impact. A prize challenge gets right at actionable solutions. I think it's really important to motivate that sort of solution-oriented thinking. Scientists don't often do a good enough job of taking research insights and packaging them into something that is practically useful.

The next step is for our solution to go from the page to the real world. When it comes to public health, there is understandable anxiety about trying new things. It's a very "if it ain't broke, don't fix it" kind of philosophy. But a system doesn't have to be broken to be improved. Water regulators want to ensure that water treatment is carried out safely. Existing monitoring methods accomplish that goal, but flow cytometry could help accomplish that goal faster, more cheaply, and more reliably.

ONE SMART CROWD

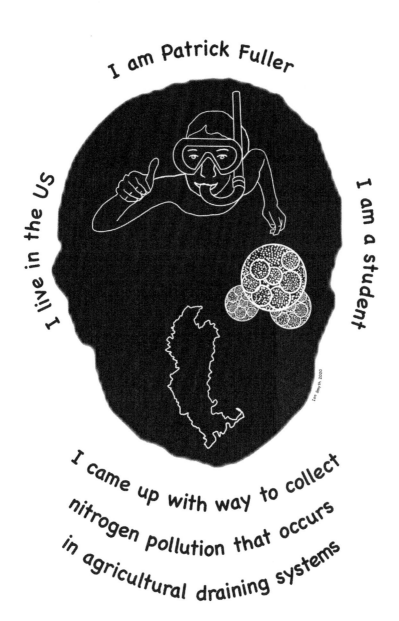

My name is Patrick Fuller - "While my academic background helped, most of the inspiration came from my upbringing."

Between 50% and 80% of fertilizer applied to commercial crops in the U.S. is not absorbed by the plants and is instead lost to water and air, causing dangerous environmental and health impacts in a growing number of watersheds around the country. A solution to capture, concentrate, or treat nitrogen pollution from agricultural field drainage is needed.

I am a PhD candidate in chemical and biological engineering at Northwestern University, collaboratively working on a variety of computational and experimental projects. This work ranges from green energy to catalysis, but all of my projects share one common goal: improving the global standard of living through the design of applied technology.

As an undergraduate, I discovered my interest in creating "actionable" technology while researching improvements in orthopedic implants. The work was very interesting, but I noticed that there was no infrastructure available to aid in converting successful research into commercial products. To fill this niche, I worked toward and obtained a second degree in finance. This business minded skillset has helped me immensely over the last few years, and I have already found myself useful as a bridge between scientific and business communities.

I took up my first challenge within a few days of discovering the platform. I was immediately drawn toward the nitrate capture problem. While my academic background helped, most of the inspiration came from my upbringing.

I was raised in a coastal New England town, where oceanography was a large portion of our grade school education. This was coupled with my experience in high school of working in a produce market, where I met farmers using nitrate-consuming algae to fertilize their crops. Following this up with some elementary reaction kinetics, I was able to devise a theoretical solution to nitrate capture.

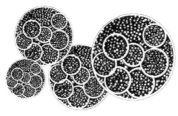

My paper proposed a solution influenced by recent advances in chemical engineering - using natural biological processes to solve synthetically rooted problems. It is a system that collects agricultural runoff in order to cultivate a nitrogen rich algae that can be reused as fertilizer. The algae can be utilized to consume pollutants in these types of drainage streams. The solution is cost-effective, environmentally friendly and was tested by Iowa soybean and corn farmers. I have since been in contact with the company, and I hope to work with them in testing and implementing my idea!

8.

There's no such thing as failure

Super Solver Nikolay Barashkov

ONE SMART CROWD

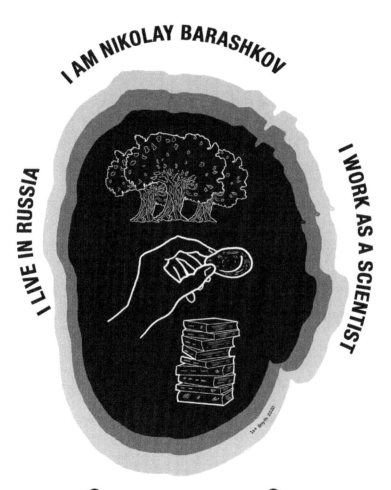

I AM NIKOLAY BARASHKOV

I LIVE IN RUSSIA

I WORK AS A SCIENTIST

I AM A SUPER SOLVER

My name is Nikolay Barashkov - "I am not sure that one should really speak of "failures" just because some proposals are not rewarded. Over the years, several dozens of my solutions have come short of winning and yet, from my personal experience, I can conclude that there is always something positive in such types of 'failure'."

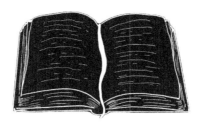

I am a scientist with 40 years of experience in polymer chemistry, photochemistry, photophysics and nanotechnology. I got my PhD in Moscow, Russia and I then moved to the US where I held positions in laboratories and universities. I'm currently a Director of R&D, however I've held numerous senior positions in R&D Departments of various industrial companies. To date I have co-written eight books (3 of which are published in English, and 5 in Russian), I have over one hundred fifty peer-reviewed papers, and hold 30 Russian, European and US Patents.

I discovered the concept of challenge prizes over 15 years ago and after browsing through the descriptions of the different innovation calls, I immediately found a challenge of interest to me. After some literature search and a fair amount of experimental work during my spare time, my original and excellent (I thought so anyway) solution was complete. I submitted it before the deadline, started to wait and… nothing happened. Months later I got a reply informing me that my solution had not been selected for the award.

Now when I look back, I am glad that this first unsuccessful attempt did not stop me from trying. To be completely honest, I had not gone back to the website for almost two years. I finally got past my initial disappointment, and submitted not one, but two more solutions. I am pleased to say that one of them, namely "Color Changing Ingredient," was a winner!

After a long career in chemical science and having worked both in academia and industry, I must confess that creative research is my passion and my addiction. Because of this, mundane everyday activities never manage to occupy my full attention. In fact, I am constantly thinking about professional challenges and consider my interaction with the platform a hobby which is closely related to my professional calling. This hobby is particularly stimulating when it gets me involved in things outside of my comfort zone. For me, a good challenge is the one which broadens your horizons. They say that "it is never too late to learn" and my experience with open innovation and crowdsourcing shows that this old saying is nothing but truth.

My favorite challenge was where a company wanted to create something unusual: a device or material that would be sensitive to touch and change its color upon gentle touch with a human finger. This so-called mechano-chromic device should NOT require any power, and the changes in color should be reversible. Well, I consider myself an expert in luminescent materials. So, my approach to the challenge was based on the principle behind a simple well-known children's toy called "Glow Slate." It is a system of at least two plastic sheets. One of them is a transparent flexible polymer sheet containing fluorescent dye or finely dispersed pigment; and the second one is a dispersive opaque sheet, like coated paper boat stock, whose smooth surface is placed adjacent to first sheet. What makes "Glow State" work is the smoothness and "wetting" properties of the sheets. The change of color, or, more exactly, the appearance of a semi-permanent luminescent image may be created by applying pressure to the first sheet with a finger. The image is stable for minutes and even hours, and it can be easily erased by separating the sheets. My secret recipe was to add some chemical reagents to both sides of the "Glow Slate". The effect of this addition lead to an interaction between the reagents. The interaction was slow enough to create a semi-permanent luminescent image but keep it "alive" for 4-5 seconds only. Within this period of time, a product of the reaction was able to separate the sides of the "Glow Slate" and the luminescent image would disappear. Then this image could be recreated by applying pressure to the surface of the modified luminescent sheet, and the cycle "appearance-disappearance" could be repeated again and again. So, while reaching this effect was not easy and the experiments required hours and hours of work in my garage temporarily converted to a testing laboratory, in the end the expectations of the company were met and my solution for this particular challenge was awarded.

For more than 12 years now, I have been invited to Kazakhstan annually to deliver university lectures to their Masters and PhD students on different topics related to polymer chemistry and nanotechnology. Whenever I come up against doubt or cynicism from my students, I always remind them of my experiences, bringing to light some of the challenges facing companies through the open innovation platform. I find that explaining some of these complex problems and going through my developed solutions in detail to be a way of demonstrating that scientific knowledge can be used to solve real world business problems.

Some of my friends, who know how much time and effort I put into projects submissions, tend to say to me: "You are not so young anymore. Why do you need to work so much? Yes, you are monetarily compensated but is the compensation worth the days and weeks of hard work over many weekends and holidays? Besides, why do you continue to go to Kazakhstan with your lectures? There are many younger knowledgeable scientists who can do it instead of you." I think to myself, I have things to accomplish and recite those lines from Robert Frost:

"The woods are lovely, dark and deep,
But I have promises to keep,
And miles to go before I sleep,
And miles to go before I sleep."

To date I've won 31 challenges and earned a decent amount of money. Nobody disagrees that money is important, but what may be even more important for me is the thrill of knowing that it was my idea that helped with a specific business problem. I am positive that all successful solvers can relate to the extraordinary feeling of having succeeded where all others failed.

What's more, I am not sure that one should really speak of "failures" just because some proposals are not rewarded. Over the years, several dozens of my solutions have come short of winning and yet, from my personal experience, I can conclude that there is always something positive in such types of "failure". From my perspective, solutions that do not receive awards are officially free from the obligations related to the intellectual property rights that otherwise would have been assigned to the company. For example, if I wish to, I can protect the research in my submission by applying for my own patents. I have submitted to the US Patent Office at least six provisional patents based on "unsuccessful" solutions. All of them were based on my rejected submissions and another one has recently been commercialized by my colleagues in Kazakhstan. In this respect, I am reminded of some lines from a Russian poet Nikolay Dorizo:

"I have lost hundred treasures and
Hundred hopes,
Nevertheless maybe all my losses
Are my major findings..."

I could not agree more with this poem. Based on my experience, I can give the following advice to anyone thinking of participating in a crowdsourcing prize challenge: Go for it, and don't be discouraged if you don't win. Try to prepare another submission and think about how your rejected solution could be implemented somewhere else.

ONE SMART CROWD

My name is Aake Staahl - "At this time of life I was what you call "fed up" with my work, and wanted to find a new way of developing my personal knowledge and I really needed something which could make my brain "wake up" again."

A company was looking to understand new potential ways to construct aqueous systems with enhanced foaming properties. Why you may ask? Well, numerous food products contain bubbles within their structure which may contribute to the texture of the product, the aroma release, the visual appearance etc. Bubbles define the texture of many commercial products that are sold aerated and are also important elements of products that are foamed in the point of consumption. Incorporating bubbles in foods is also a way to reduce their Calorie density. This was a really interested topic and it immediately intrigued me.

I am 50 years old and I live with my wife in our house in a small village in Sweden. Our three children moved out a few years ago. I am a food chemical engineer with extensive experience in the food manufacturing process like quality control, research, processing and raw material chemistry.

While reading a magazine, I came across an article about this new way of doing product developments. I became curious about it and went to the website to see what it was. I found it very interesting, and the chance to win a great reward if my proposal was chosen, made me shiver. How exciting! This was an opportunity to show your competence, work with your brain without limitations and compete with others to find the best solution and get money for it! I was immediately hooked on the idea and signed up right away.

At this time of life I was what you call "fed up" with my work, and wanted to find a new way of developing my personal knowledge and I really needed something which could make my brain "wake up" again. This platform turned out to be this injection! I thought many times that my employer did not fully use my knowledge and competence in their business. Now suddenly an opportunity popped up for me to let the creative part of my brain operate again and at the same time being able to do the regular work for my employer. This problem-solving side could be done in my spare time after work. An extra 'hobby-work', so to say.

I started to send in submissions, which I personally thought were very good, but was rejected for various reasons. This did not stop me, as I was eager to learn and succeed. Suddenly, without really believing it, I received a positive message explaining that my solution had been positively evaluated and had become the winning solution! I could not believe that little old me had won! I was very happy about this and took all the required documents for the "due diligence process" to my employer to sign to verify that the suggestion was not anything which they had the intellectual property on. Now the real problems started!

Even though all the work I had been done outside of work and outside my business area, my employers refused to sign the papers! After a process with the board of the company we came to an agreement and my papers were finally signed and I got my award. Shortly after this I saw the stable emulsion challenge and immediate thought "I know the solution to this!"

Wise from experience, I contacted my employer before I contributed, submitted my proposed solution, and it turned out that I was awarded for the second time! I could not have imagined I would win again! Now all the mental barriers I had about the possibility of me and my skills to solve such challenges have fallen. I now think it can happen again, and again!

ONE SMART CROWD

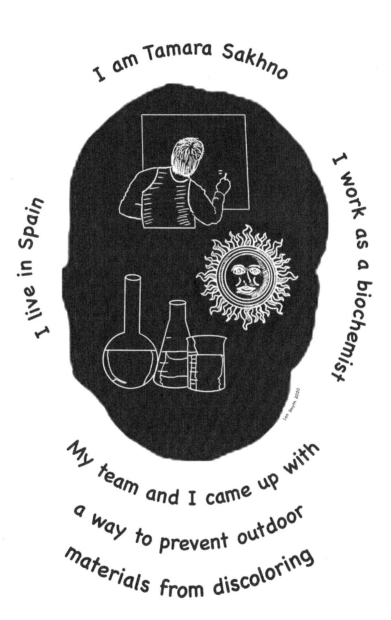

I am Tamara Sakhno

I work as a biochemist

I live in Spain

My team and I came up with a way to prevent outdoor materials from discoloring

Ian Smyth 2020

My name is Tamara Sakhno - "The two things I love about the open innovation model is gaining practical knowledge about real life problems and realizing that if I'm awarded for the solution I provided, the company will be using MY solution in practical application. "

A company that produces materials for outdoor use is finding that the product changes from its original color due to exposure to humidity and sunlight over time. The company was seeking novel ideas to reduce degradation of the material in these conditions by coming up with an additive to stabilize the color of its material and prevent discoloration. The materials in question are formulations made of oil, resin, and polymers and it is believed that it is the reactive aromatic and polyaromatic compounds found in oils and resins that are driving the discoloration.

The first time I heard about the open innovation business model a while back via a former colleague who was already an active member of the open innovation community. I was skeptical in the beginning, but surprisingly, after working on a solution with colleagues, our solution was selected for an award. After that, I was part of a group that submitted 6 solutions for different problems and 3 of them won!

My favorite challenge was one whereby the company was searching for ways to prevent the discoloration of materials that had been exposed to light and humidity. I should mention that protection of polymer-based material from sunlight was a part of my dissertation for my doctorate degree over 20 years ago. However, my experience in the field of light stabilizers and particularly in stabilization of colored polymers by using the quenchers of singlet oxygen seemed to be useful in this case. We found out that the synergistic effect of free radical capturing and singlet oxygen quenching was what made our submission unique. We hope that the company was able to use the synergy I mentioned in practical implementation of our approach to improving the lifetime of colored polymer-based coatings.

In another challenge, the company was searching for a technology to limit the diffusion rate of micro-encapsulated disaccharides (simple sugars, soluble in water), like lactose and sucrose, in aqueous solutions. Microencapsulation technology is used for providing stability of the active ingredient in food products, and in this case the challenge focused on limiting the rate of diffusion of these simple sugars when places in an aqueous solution (e.g. water). The difficult parts of this problems included not only significantly decreasing the rate of dissolution disaccharides, but also the expectations that the proposed material should be allowed for use in foods. Our literature analysis showed that there are dozens of polymer-based materials that are capable to limit the diffusion rate from microcapsules, however, 99% of them were not designed for use in food products. Without disclosing the exact chemical nature of polymer systems we proposed, I will mention only that we were able to find a cellulose derivative cross-linked by one of polyvalent metal salts (both components are food grade) which shows the satisfactory performance under rather demanding conditions indicated by the Seeker.

I have submitted 7 solutions so far, and my "success rate" has been just slightly below 50%. I like to work with the chemical literature so, my main contribution in all three winning solutions was the literature search which allowed our team to provide the most detailed description of the "state of the art", so to speak. I should admit that the main ideas of winning solutions were not mine however, both of us perfectly realize that our awarded solutions were products of our synergistic efforts.

I'm currently teaching chemistry, biochemistry and related fields in two Universities located in Poltava, Ukraine. Sometimes my students have a certain skepticism regarding the applicability of the academic knowledge I'm trying to deliver to their attention in their every day life. In the cases when my solutions were accepted and awarded, I like to describe to my students the technical problems faced by certain companies and the nature of my solutions proposed for resolving these particular technical problems. I strongly believe that "teaching by example" is more productive than any other type of teaching.

The two things I love about the open innovation model is gaining practical knowledge about real life problems and realizing that if I'm awarded for the solution I provided, the company will be using MY solution in practical application. This knowledge makes me proud and its even better that I get a financial award from my service.

My advice is that no one should be discouraged from the lack of immediate success in submitted solutions. It is a competitive process but with each submission you learn and get something out of it – so keep trying!

ONE SMART CROWD

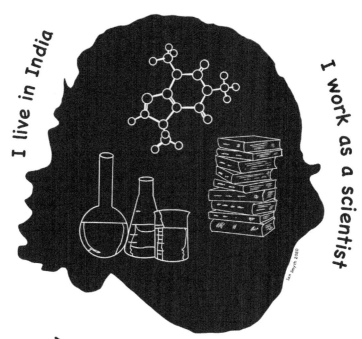

I am Dr Ammanamanchi Radhakrishna

I live in India

I work as a scientist

I have solved challenges for protein crosslinks, combinatorial polypeptides and tanning compounds

My name is Ammanamanchi Radhakrishna - "In my opinion, it does not require special skills to solve problems. What is does require is critical creativity, understanding the challenge and joining the ends for successful solution."

My open innovation journey started in 2003 with the discovery of a new pharmaceutical compound that can help restore the body to a more 'youthful' state to combat the causes of aging.

Glucosepane is a protein crosslink that causes stiffening of various body parts and reduces elasticity throughout the body. Evidence suggests that glucosepane may play a role in osteoporosis and cardiovascular diseases like hypertension, inflammation and diabetes. Scientists have studied the accumulation of glucosepane for 30 years with little success. A company seeking innovative ideas to biologically reverse one of the causes of aging and age-related diseases believed to be attributed to glucosepane.

My 35-year scientific career has given me the passion for creative approaches to solving complex research problems. I have contributed to the development of more than 40 chemical process discoveries, which have been commercialized and capitalized by various industries. My major scientific fields of interests are natural products, synthetic organic chemistry, biopolymers, heterocyclic chemistry, analytical research, drug development, new polymer formulations, biotechnology, proteomics, disease biomarker development, biodegradable polyolefins, and chem-bio informatics. I have been author and co-author of 18 scientific publications and also hold 7 national and international patents.

When I came across the open innovation platform in 2003, it sparked my interest and I submitted a solution for the "Protein Crosslinks" problem with a hypothesis in my mind and a few days of library work. The main challenge for me was the thought process and decoding the challenge details. Once this was in place, connecting the solution gaps was the next challenge which requires knowledge, skills, experience, and literature work. My rich experience in the pharmaceutical drug development made it easy to fill the gaps and create the solution for my first solution award.

Glycation and protein crosslink's have been implicated as strong contributors to many progressive diseases of aging including vascular diseases such as hypertension, poor capillary circulation, kidney disease, stiffness of joints and skin, cataracts, Alzheimer's, dementia etc. My solution to these biological problems yielded a new class of pharmaceutical compounds that can break the established Advanced Glycation End Products (AGEs) crosslinks and restore the physiological system back into a more 'youthful' state of biological process elasticity or lost functions. At the time, I was hoping that one day these miracle compounds would be an alternative to the avoid the complicated surgical procedures and medical treatment of glycation related issues, through simple drug therapy.

As I submitted my solution, though I was confident, I was not sure how it would be received or evaluated. However, when I received confirmation that my solution has been selected for full award I was delighted!

In the subsequent four years I've had 10 unsuccessful attempts to win another award, but it has not stopped my creativity or drive to submit open innovation solution. I am pleased, today that I have 19 successful awards from InnoCentive and 5 from other open innovation platforms. My experience with this particular open innovation platform and community has been highly rewarding scientifically and financially. In my opinion, it does not require special skills to solve problems. What is does require is critical creativity, understanding the challenge and joining the ends for successful solution. One should be addicted to the scientific thought process for getting their ideas in-front of others to be successful.

I am amazed by the success of open innovation and the global shift in the approach to R&D lead generation and success. Today open innovation business models are shaping new ways of research and intellectual innovation opportunities are being administered to solve large global issues. I strongly support open innovation for areas of global concern such as: Food sustainability, Climate Change, Global warming control, Marine Pollution, Marine Crop Cultivation for Novel Chemical and Food Source as alternative to land cultivation, Social Security, Health Care, Global Economy, Space Debris Control, Human Skill Development, Artificial Intelligence, Alternative Energy and Energy Efficiency. I think there is a great opportunity for novel ideas and businesses models in these areas to convert complex problems into simple creative solutions to contribute to the much-needed global outlook change for research, development and innovation.

I'm currently working on two life ambition projects "Efforts to Understand the Life Language Code" and "Environmentally Biodegradable Polyolefin Polymers" with a team of young scientific minds. My goal is to bring about innovation, new ideas, solutions and leads for the development of science that has high impact on a large section of mankind and potential societal problems. I enjoy solving difficult problems, particularly those that require cross-pollination from one field to another.

ONE SMART CROWD

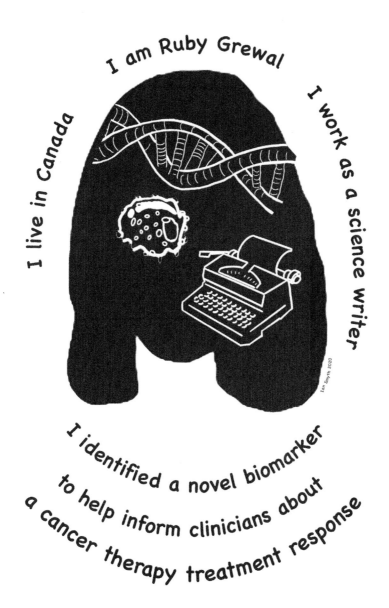

I am Ruby Grewal

I work as a science writer

I live in Canada

I identified a novel biomarker to help inform clinicians about a cancer therapy treatment response

Ian Smyth 2020

My name is Ruby Grewal - "I first discovered the open innovation business in a profile in a magazine. I had been involved in science research before becoming a science writer and was interested in continuing to participate in research."

Bevacizumab is an anti-angiogenesis biological therapy used in cancer treatment. To date the drug has been used to treat more than 2.2 million patients worldwide. Bevacizumab blocks blood vessel growth to cancer cells through the Vascular Endothelial Growth Factor (VEGF) pathway. The goal of this challenge is to find a novel biomarker that can be used to inform clinicians whether patients are more or less likely to benefit from anti-tumor treatment with bevacizumab.

I first discovered the open innovation business in a profile in a magazine. I had been involved in science research before becoming a science writer and was interested in continuing to participate in research. I have a Bachelor of Science in genetics and have also conducted medical research as a PhD candidate. There are many genetic components to disease treatment and treatment response. I examined the published literature on genetic mutations to understand how they may affect treatment response.

I have been an avid supporter of the platform for over 10 years. Over this time I have worked on 42 submissions and been awarded 8 challenges ranging from exploring novel biomarkers, researching clinical trials and viral pathogens to discovering food grade materials or formulations that can be used to replace gelatin and that are not derived from animal sources.

One specific challenge that stands out to me was one that asked for identification of novel biomarkers for bevacizumab treatment response. Bevacizumab is an anti-angiogenesis biological therapy used in cancer treatment. It blocks blood vessel growth to cancer cells through the VEGF pathway. However, there are certain mutations present in up to 50% of cancer patients (depending on cancer type), that result in increased signaling through different pathways. These other pathways don't respond to bevacizumab treatment, and therefore patients with these mutations may not respond to this treatment, which would result in decreased bevacizumab efficacy. The premise of my awarded submission was that the identified genetic mutations may be novel biomarkers of bevacizumab treatment response.

It would be ideal if I could stay involved with the research solution and its further development. I would also like to see if the theoretical approaches I propose can be verified by research. I think for me the end to end approach would be really beneficial, to see what happens after the submission, or to stay involved in the process to see the idea come into fruition. It would also be great to have the ability to look at winning solutions, to see how others approach the problems. I will continue to monitor medical and biological challenges in the future as I enjoy the opportunity to stay engaged in research and learning about new research areas.

ONE SMART CROWD

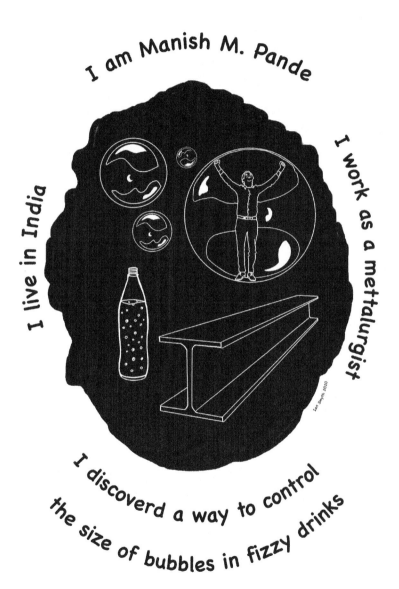

My name is Manish M. Pande - "I feel that every problem posted is an opportunity for the Solvers to push their thinking limits and come out with a solution that is of real practical significance."

The soft drink market is highly competitive, with revenue amounting to over $600 million in 2020. The ability to control and manipulate the physical characteristics of bubbles in soft drinks is directly correlated with beverage quality. Smaller bubbles contribute to higher acceptability of drink. The seeker company is interested in altering the size of the bubbles in their soft drinks. Ideas for changing or manipulating bubbles through ingredients or packaging of the product are needed.

I am a metallurgist by profession; a materials scientist specializing in iron and steel. I obtained my bachelors and master's degree in Metallurgical Engineering. I spent nearly three and half years in the steel industry in operations and R&D before starting my PhD.

When I came across the problem controlling bubble sizes in fizzy drinks it interested me. I had previously worked on metallic foams during my master's thesis and I also had a basic knowledge about the physics of foaming of metals. I proposed a method to manipulate the characteristics of bubbles in carbonated beverage and I was ecstatic to learn that the proposed method turned out to be the winning solution!

I feel that every problem is an opportunity for people like me to push their thinking limits and come out with a solution that is of real practical significance. The statistics shows that there are hundreds of thousands of self-titled problem solvers from all over the world who have developed their thinking and approach to problems in different educational environments. In such a scenario, even the participation of 0.001% submissions for any problem, makes it truly competitive.

In this tough competition, proposing the right solution is no mean feat. Especially because in many cases the seeker company has already exhausted all the possible resources in their disposal. It makes winning a challenge even sweeter and instills confidence in your abilities.

9.

Stay hungry, stay foolish

Super Solver Ted Ground

ONE SMART CROWD

I AM TED GROUND

I LIVE IN TEXAS, USA

I WORK IN CONSULTANCY

I AM A
SUPER SOLVER

<u>My name is Ted Ground</u> - "When working on solutions, solitude is important. Take walks in the woods, or on the beach. Take a bike ride. Spend a day in the library, alone. Reading books, and remembering news articles and books that you have read, years ago, seems to help - a lot!"

I am a 5th generation Texan - my ancestors settled in Texas in 1848. I have 4 exceptional children, and 4 wonderful grandchildren. While I have traveled some, to a tolerable degree, I plan to live the rest of my life here in Texas, where my grandchildren live. I earned my Bachelor of Science degree in Biology and several years later, I earned my Master's degree in Aquatic Biology at Texas State University writing a thesis about water quality in freshwater reservoirs of Texas.

As a technical writer and consultant for many different projects, I have been self-employed for much of my career. I have worked in positions related to natural resources, environmental science, and analytical instrument labs, up to management levels. I've also been in technical sales for water filtration and process control equipment companies. At a young age, I plowed fields with our farm tractors, I hauled hay, worked in carpentry, and general construction. I mention this only because I think it is more important to try to do things, and to make things, than it is to just think about things. But "access to tools" is necessary.

I have broad interests in science and technology, from astronomy to zoology. Innovations in specialized fields, such as aerospace propulsion, aquaculture, and geothermal, nuclear, and solar energy, capture my attention. I am fascinated by exploration and commercial development of the solar system. But, back here on Earth, I am interested in reversing desertification with developments in solar thermal desalination, and sustainable agriculture's role in that, tied to soil conservation, and managed grazing.

Expertise is a moving target to aim for. We learn from research and experience, apply what we learn, and then, from refining those applications, we learn more, in a continuous process. To continue learning new things, thinking about new ways of doing things, and actually doing them, is part of a rewarding life. It can keep me busy and balanced, passing time with pastimes, which is all I have left here!

You might say that I was recruited to the platform by roving "curiosity". The first problem that I ever tackled was the Mars Balance Mass challenge. The idea for a solution struck me immediately, with some help from watching the clouds at sunset. I sat at my computer keyboard, on a workbench and makeshift desk, in the laundry room of my brother's farmhouse, near Rising Star, Texas, where I lived for several years. It was a good place to think, and to write. In about a week I had it written up, with cited references, and drafted graphics, to illustrate my idea. Solitude helped fuel and feed my one-man army on a solitary march – a party of one, and a Lone Star R&D think tank. Over the next year, I would write 68 of "my ideas" there, at that simple desk, made of painted plywood and lumber.

It would be months before I was notified about NASA's evaluations. In the meantime, I pressed on, trying my hand at 9 other challenges despite having learned nothing about winning or losing the NASA Challenge. I've no clue what motivated me to continue writing, except that engaging in these pastimes was its own reward.

Later that year, I won my first award, for "Identifying Novel Sources of Trace Minerals". It was totally unexpected news. It was great to win an award of $5,000, out of a $7,000 prize pool - I had won first place - Merry Christmas! It encouraged me to continue to enter, when and if I could, other challenges that I felt comfortable enough to try to compose ideas for. Later, that would change, as I tried my hand at composing ideas that "pushed the envelope" of my comfort zone.

Then, in early January, I was very surprised to read receive this email:

> Dear Ted, It gives me great pleasure to let you know that the Seeker's review of your submission to InnoCentive 9933607 – NASA's Balance Mass Challenge: Using "Dead Weight" on Mars Spacecraft to Advance Science and Technology - led to a favorable evaluation. You will be awarded a total of $20,000. The Seeker has provided you with the following feedback.

> "This submission is an extremely well-thought out concept with very creative use of the Balance Mass Devices which would meet technical requirements. Good use of citations and historical comparison to sounding rocket investigations. What made this submission stand out was its simplicity and practicality with a potentially high yield in scientific knowledge. Little to no modification of the Mars Science Laboratory re-entry system would be

required. Concept warrants further investigation into the availability of orbital and ground assets and feasibility of obtaining the desired data on the release of barium and/ or other tracer elements. It is the opinion of the Balance Challenge review team that this challenge clearly stood out from the rest of the submissions and has been approved for the full $20,000 award. Congratulations for the creative thinking and useful solution!"

I was also invited to give a presentation to the scientists and engineers at the Jet Propulsion Laboratory (JPL) in Pasadena, California later that year. I had hoped that my solution would have been used for the next NASA rover mission to land on Mars - named "Perseverance". Underway now, it's scheduled to land on Mars on February 18, 2021. Although it seemed to have been favorably welcomed at the presentation that I gave at the Jet Propulsion Laboratory (JPL), unfortunately, it was not included in that mission. I try to follow news of that mission closely. Perhaps there is still hope that some version of my idea will be used in other, future missions to Mars, or even to Titan, since that moon of Saturn also has an atmosphere that calls for further observation and study. I hope so – for even more fun and novelty to help pass our time with!

It was only much later that I learned that there were 2,138 active solvers, with 219 proposals submitted from 43 countries. I was again very surprised that I won first place, or any award, with that level of competition.

One interesting thing to me is that many of my ideas existed in some form, before I ever learned or read about a particular challenge. For example, I have often wondered or day-dreamed about the atmosphere of Mars, or what polymers and composites could be made by "In-Situ Resource Utilization" (ISRU) of materials available on Mars. And, I have often wondered about finding better, more efficient, and less costly ways to desalinate water to help reverse desertification right here on good old Mother Earth. Sometimes it takes a challenge to come along and offer a game prize – an incentive to polish up, formalize, and articulate old antique ideas that I may have pondered, but were put on the shelf, years before.

I have only won about 24% of the challenges I have participated in, so I do not consider this a job or career. Solvers, or, players if you will, submit their intellectual property (ideas) as individual sellers in a kind of marketplace, with something like "game rules", but there are significant differences. They may choose to sell products of creativity, and some, all, or none of their proprietary rights. It's like holding a garage sale from time to time, in which businesses are "bargain hunters" shopping for products (ideas, or rights to use ideas) to buy from a Solver who may or may not agree to sell, for a certain price, perhaps some "old stuff" that has been cleaned up and polished a bit, for "curbside appeal". There is some room for "price negotiation", in a few cases. Each challenge is a separate pastime activity for me, but this is not a consistent hobby, as I define it. They are like word puzzles – but each is different and unique, and there may be more than one "right" set of answers or words that fit the puzzle, to win awards. That's why there are often multiple individual winners, with different solutions, for any given challenge. These marketplace activities are distinct from games of chance, in that they involve more than just random chance or probability - there's no betting, so this isn't gambling, either. Although there may be some guesswork.

Some of my ideas existed before I ever learned of a particular challenge. Some ideas are still "on the shelf" and may never be "sold" or patented. I wonder if some ideas are really new (novel), since "there is nothing new under the sun", as they say. More like antiques with a previous owner, who is himself an antique, some ideas are relics from a different age. Novelty or innovation might be created by using those old ideas, but in new ways. I might recall a 50-year old patent for a device to use in a new way to develop an "Environmentally Friendly Replacement for Buoy Mooring Systems", as in a challenge some years back. Sometimes, old dogs can teach you new tricks.

When working on solutions, solitude is important. Take walks in the woods, or on the beach. Take a bike ride. Spend a day in the library, alone. Reading books, and remembering news articles and books that you have read, years ago, seems to help - a lot! Even if it turns out that your memory is not 100% accurate, it might hint at a connection, so go back and check it out. How might it be connected? I often think of something that I read 50 or more years ago, such as the case of the Whole Earth Catalog.

Around the time I was 12 to 14 years old, I was introduced to the Whole Earth Catalog. The by-line of that seminal publication was "Access to Tools". It was about learning more about Whole Systems, especially ecosystems. The Whole Earth Catalog, was also about self-empowerment, and greater self-reliance, and "alternative" energy, that folks could gather from the environment at their own homestead: solar, wind, water, biomass. I was all about that. It literally changed my life and made an impression on me at that age.

Someone once said that the Whole Earth Catalog was the internet before the internet. Please check out A Short History of the Whole Earth Catalog I especially like this quote from Steve Jobs from that article:

> "When I was young, there was an amazing publication called the Whole Earth Catalog, which was one of the bibles of my generation. It was created by a fellow named Stewart Brand not far from here in Menlo Park, and he brought it to life with his poetic touch. This was in the late 1960s, before personal computers and desktop publishing, so it was all made with typewriters, scissors and Polaroid cameras. It was sort of like Google in paperback form, 35 years before Google came along: it was idealistic, and overflowing with neat tools and great notions….

> Stewart and his team put out several issues of the Whole Earth Catalog, and then, when it had run its course, they put out a final issue. It was the mid-1970s, and I was your age. On the back

cover of their final issue was a photograph of an early morning country road, the kind you might find yourself hitchhiking on if you were so adventurous. Beneath it were the words "Stay hungry. Stay foolish". It was their farewell message as they signed off. Stay hungry. Stay foolish. And I have always wished that for myself. And now, as you graduate to begin anew, I wish that for you. Stay hungry. Stay foolish."

I would never have expected that I would submit as many proposals as I have to date. As of this writing, I have completed 93 challenge proposals, and I have won 22 of them. Those 93 challenge proposals, or ideas, total 2,205 pages, so the average is 20 - 25 pages, while one was 96 pages. A few years ago, I was sending in my ideas about once every 2-3 weeks. At my advanced age, I've slowed down some.

So, go on a long, slow walk, or a bike ride, and watch the clouds glow in a sunset, deep in the heart of Texas, or wherever you happen to hang your hat.

ONE SMART CROWD

I am Thomas Stowe

I work as a consultant

I live in the US

I came up with a way to increase light passing through glasses lenses

Ian Smyth 2020

My name is Thomas Stowe - "I'm nothing if not obsessed with information and knowledge — I've become quite savvy when it comes to informatics and data mining because of these passions."

Polycarbonate is a light weight, exceptionally durable plastic often used for eye lenses. Polycarbonate is about 10 times stronger than glass or regular plastic and was originally invented in the process of creating astronaut visors. A company is searching for ideas for new ways of increasing the refractive index of polycarbonate. Refractive index, also called index of refraction, is a measure of the bending of a ray of light when passing from one medium into another. Knowing the refractive indices of different media helps to identify the direction in which way the light would bend while passing from one medium to another.

I'm a twenty-something year old Texan with heavy interests in science and engineering. My favorite educational past-time is studying statistics relating to various markets and economic trends. My hobbies are researching historical sites and scouting for artifacts with my metal detectors, spending time with my wife at parks and enjoying rural and natural environments. I try to keep abreast of technology trends, science news and keep informed on matters relevant to my interests.

I stumbled upon the open innovation website while looking for knowledge markets. I've been successful in selling my skills and expertise in the past and once I found knowledge markets, I found that what I had to contribute was very much acknowledged and appreciated. I'm nothing if not obsessed with information and knowledge — I've become quite savvy when it comes to informatics and data mining because of these passions.

I decided to work on a project after a water cooler discussion with my colleagues about the platform. The idea of winning the amount paid for most solutions which is between $1,000 – $20,000+ made the geeky people I work with drool. I like to help people find opportunities. Whether it's a sure-fire telecommuting job to supplementing savings in between employers, or a cheap small business project they can undertake with little money in their spare time. I like the response I get when I present 110% real, concrete concepts that have been tested by myself and others.

I'm spending a little more than half ($600) of the $1,000 prize money awarded to me on IT certifications that I've been wanting for a while. I hope these new credentials will allow me to find a better paying position. I'm spending the rest of the money augmenting my swing trading account. I've been trading stocks for the past month and I'm up 300%. This new capital will hopefully enable me to turn that $400 into $2,000 in one month.

I donated another $1000 from a different challenge I won to a cause that is local to me and dear to my heart. Born to Read is a charity run by an organization in Bexar County, Texas providing 25,000 bilingual literacy kits, one to every baby born in Bexar County. These kits include 2 books (1 bilingual), a library card application and helpful tips on how to raise a reader. I donated this money on behalf of my mother and sent this personalized note on behalf of my brother and myself. "Mom – you managed to give my brother and I joy and later hope to read, learn, gain skills and stand on our own. I hope that we achieve more than you prayed for. With Love, On behalf of Jerome and I"

Without my mother and her passion for reading and learning, not to mention supplying us with books and educational tools (computers, art supplies, typewriters), my brother and I would have been educationally bereft. My mother enabled me to pursue any subject that interested me and showed me how to teach myself. Luckily, I've found a wife that's just as encouraging. They both definitely approve of my donation

I've recently started plans for creating and owning a small business, following in the footsteps of my mother and grandmother. I have achieved great progress recently and my life keeps getting better but more importantly, my long-term goals are becoming closer and more attainable.

ONE SMART CROWD

I am David Bradin

I work as a patent lawyer

I live in the US

I invented an innovative synthesis of butane tetracarboxylic acid

Ian Smyth 2020

My name is David Bradin - "I quickly realized that the solution could be made using a reaction that few chemists know about, but that I would never forget."

The Seeker company is searching for an efficient synthetic route to mass-produce a specific molecular substance, in this case butane tetracarboxylic acid (BTCA), using readily available raw materials. This material is useful in the durable press finishing of perma press fabrics. Several synthetic approaches have been reported in the literature for BTCA, however, available preparations were expensive and as such not viable for large scale production. The goal was to define the best synthetic pathway using scalable reagents and raw materials. The proposed route had to be amenable to large scale production on the order of several thousand tons of product per year and the approach must be cost effective.

I work as a patent lawyer, primarily focusing on pharmaceuticals, petroleum chemistry, polymer chemistry and biotechnology. I have assisted clients in developing world-wide patent strategies, drafted and procured patents in the US and coordinated patent procurement worldwide.

I was one of the initial problem solvers in the very early days. While browsing the website, I scrolled down the list of problems, and saw one where the answer immediately popped into my head, based on a prior experience I had as a chemist before going to law school.

Back then, I was working as a process development chemist. I was involved in the large-scale synthesis of a severe lachrymator (i.e., tear gas), and when my synthesis was scaled from the bench scale to the 1000-gallon scale, one of the operators forgot to turn on the cooling tower. The reactor overheated, and produced a by-product that caused the tear gas to go off-spec. With 1000 gallons of tear gas in the reactor, I had to find a way to identify and remove the impurities. This took the better part of four days, during which time I characterized the impurities, determined how they were formed and what properties they had, and tried about every possible way to remove them. I ended up sleeping on my desk a few nights, getting very little sleep over that period. Eventually, we improved the purity enough that we were able to sell the compound.

That Friday, I was supposed to go to a Grateful Dead concert with my then girlfriend and some friends of mine from grad school. My friends had the tickets and were in a separate car, which my girlfriend and I were to follow. My girlfriend was driving, and I fell fast asleep unexpectedly, only to wake up after my girlfriend lost sight of my friend with the tickets. I never ended up seeing the concert. In any event, I've never forgotten the chemistry that resulted in this unfortunate side effect. So, when I saw the problem posted, I did a retrosynthetic analysis of the compound at issue, and quickly realized that it could be made using a reaction that few chemists know about, but that I would never forget because of my experience.

It actually took me more time to register on the platform than it took to win the challenge. I still recall receiving three e-mails on a Sunday, advising me that I had won. My wife and I had just shopped for a new kitchen floor, and the estimated cost was, almost to the penny, the amount of the award money.

Over my time, I've had some amazing experiences as part of the Solver community. Perhaps because I'm not a full-time practicing chemist, I've been interviewed by some of my favorite magazines, newspapers, and journals, including MIT Technology Review, Chemical and Engineering News, Forbes, Business Week, Business 2.0, and the Boston Globe, to name a few. I've had people I know tell me that they also tried to solve the same problem, and a few clients have approached me to say that they've read that I won a challenge. I was interviewed on NPR, and a lot of my family, friends, and clients heard the interview. I was invited to give a lecture on crowdsourcing at one of Europe's leading business schools in Lausanne, Switzerland. Needless to say, my experiences have been very rewarding, personally as well as financially.

In my profession, I've seen that there are two types of patent lawyers – lawyers who happen to have a science background, and scientists who happen to have a law background. I consider myself the latter. This is part of the reason I really enjoy looking at the challenges posted. Although I haven't submitted a putative solution in a while, I have scoured for others where I might have a "flash of insight." I still read up on many of chemistry problems posted because trying to solve them makes me feel like a chemist again. I'm sure that sounds a bit corny, but it's true.

"It took me more time to register as a Solver than it took to win the challenge."

ONE SMART CROWD

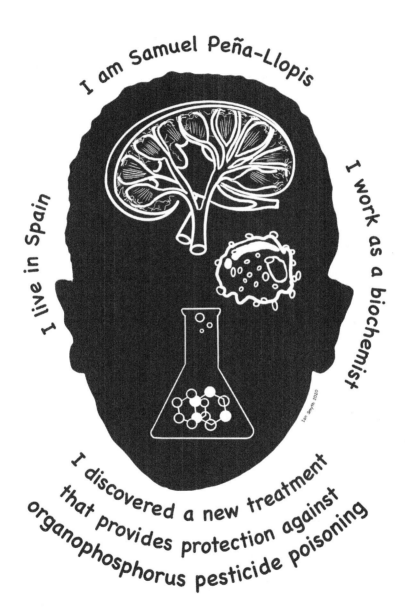

I am Samuel Peña-Llopis

I work as a biochemist

I live in Spain

I discovered a new treatment that provides protection against organophosphorus pesticide poisoning

Ian Smyth 2020

My name is Samuel Peña-Llopis - "Open innovation offers a new way of solving problems and at the end, innovation promotes the progress of our society. For me it is very rewarding to be part of the journey."

Currently more than 100 different organophosphorus pesticides (OP) are used as insecticides in agriculture and gardening. The number of intoxications with OP pesticides is estimated at 3 million per year and the number of deaths and casualties at around 300,000 per year worldwide. A new approach is needed to provide enhanced protection against OP poisoning.

I was born and raised in Castellón, Spain. I grew up interested in science, as my father is a biologist and my mother a chemistry teacher. I obtained a degree in biochemistry from the University of Barcelona. While earning my Ph.D. at the University of Valencia, I was privileged to be mentored by a remarkable researcher, as well as my own father, who allowed me to open my own research line at the Spanish National Research Council (CSIC).

While studying there on the mechanisms of resistance to oxidative stress and pesticides, I realized that innovation was a crucial aspect of science and I began looking for applications for my research. That work led to a couple of patents and several papers, one of which received a distinguished award. A few months after defending my PhD, I received a postdoctoral fellowship to study the effects of oxidative stress on gene regulation at Harvard University. After that, I got the chance to lead a project to uncover the molecular events driving kidney cancer.

My own family, like many others, has directly felt the devastating effects of cancer. Though I could not help my brother, I have the satisfaction of discovering one of the main genes involved in kidney cancer. When mutated, it leads to higher aggressive tumors and poor patient survival. These findings enable patient stratification and precision medicine in renal cell carcinoma. We are currently trying to identify in my lab new therapeutic opportunities, which someday might benefit patients.

The first time I came across the OP poisoning problem, it immediately got my attention because I knew a good answer to the question that it asked. I was very confident of winning, since I recently wrote a review article about exactly the same topic: the use of antioxidants and, specifically, glutathione pro-drugs, such as N-acetylcysteine, to boost OP detoxification and counteract the oxidative stress caused by pesticides. Thus, it took me a relatively short time to prepare the submission, because I previously invested a significant amount of time in writing the review. Overall, antioxidants can provide both protection and treatment against OP poisoning with less side effects than other drugs.

Open innovation offers a new way of solving problems and at the end, innovation promotes the progress of our society. For me it is very rewarding to be part of the journey.

ONE SMART CROWD

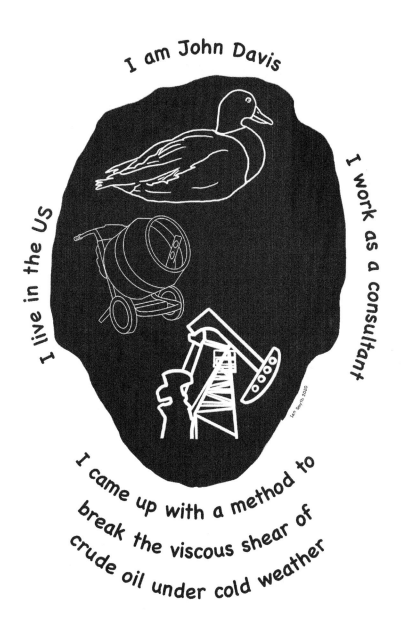

My name is John Davis - "I came up with a method to break the viscous shear of crude oil under cold weather conditions helping to clean up a 20 year old oil spill from the 1989 Exxon Valdez disaster."

The Exxon Valdez oil spill was a manmade disaster that occurred when Exxon Valdez, an oil tanker owned by the Exxon Shipping Company, spilled 11 million gallons of crude oil into Alaska's Prince William Sound on March 24, 1989. The Oil Spill Recovery Institute (OSRI) was established by Congress in response to the 1989 Exxon Valdez oil spill. Oil slick covered 1,300 miles of coastline and killed hundreds of thousands of seabirds, otters, seals and whales.

By 2007, in the aftermath of the Exxon Valdez oil spill, there were still over 120,000 liters of oil trapped in the Alaskan coastline and surrounding seas. The OSRI sought to clean-up after the Exxon Valdez oil spill and posed a challenge to the global solver community to find a method to separate oil from water; specifically oil that had solidified into a viscous mass with frozen water in recovery barges.

My name is John Davis and I studied chemistry at Illinois State University and the University of Notre Dame. I have worked as a consultant for petrochemical and general manufacturing facilities, but like most people, I have previously had many different kinds of jobs. One summer, I gained some experience in construction pouring concrete, and I used some of that knowledge to help inspire and solve a problem that would enable crude oil (from oil spills) to be removed from arctic waters.

Concrete vibrators are used to allow the concrete mixture to easily flow into smaller cracks and crevices when forming concrete and can also be used to restore liquid flow to concrete that has begun to set-up prematurely. The first time I saw this in action, I was completely amazed. The concrete vibrator was like a magic wand; when merely touched to a tall mound of setting concrete, it restored flow so quickly that it actually splashed back down to ground level. I realized that with some minor modifications, pneumatic concrete vibrators could resolve the issue by restoring liquid flow to the icy oil slush mixture.

When I was writing up my solution, I thought that perhaps this solution was too obvious. Slushy frozen oil-sea water mixtures in sub-arctic waters behave very similar to fresh poured (uncured) cement, for which a concrete vibrator is used to allow it to flow more freely. My solution was to use modified pneumatic concrete vibrators to keep the oil-water slush moving with more fluidity. Certainly, others would have tried this already! However, it turned out that this unique tool of the concrete industry, as applied to an oil industry problem, had not yet been explored. It is a perfect illustration of how seeking input outside of the usual channels to solve a problem can lead to new insights and discoveries that may otherwise have been missed.

Like many others, I enjoy the challenge of solving problems. And, helping to tackle this major environmental problem was particularly satisfying. It means a lot to me that I made a contribution which is being used by the OSRI, because their work is very important. In fact, the prize money has been utilized primarily to finance the exploration of other high impact innovations, including other environmental and soil remediation technologies. I plan to visit OSRI in Alaska to watch my solution in action someday.

ONE SMART CROWD

I am Anonymous

I have solved a number of problems

I am Anonymous

For personal reasons, I am not ready to reveal my identity in open and I have worked anonymously through the platform, like many other Solvers, who have preferred such a variant.

I am a professional organic chemist, with a PhD and also have a keen interest in other chemistry-related fields as well. However, the town I live in is located outside of notable chemical centers in our country, and for this reason my current work is not related to my profession. It's because of this that the chemistry-based challenges posted on the platform are of interest to me professionally, and provides a way to demonstrate my expertise in these fields. Chemical challenges are for me both a hobby and career, which help me to test myself and self-educate while working on new challenges. Lots of the new challenges posted also indicate the current trends, which are happening right now in the world.

I first discovered the platform online. I was immediately intrigued by the chemical and biological challenges, and I decided to test myself and to take a part out of curiosity. The first challenge which I entered was related to a synthesis of Pyrrolo-Pyrimidine. I suggested several possible routes to the given molecule in my submission but I did not win because it was a RTP (Reduction to Practice) challenge so I needed to find a prototype that showed my ideas in practice and my solution was fully theoretical. Because of this, I lost interest in the platform some years after that and was not aware of many of the interesting challenges that were published during this period.

My favorite challenges are those where I feel that I can suggest something new or something better than many other Solvers could suggest. There are many challenges related to developing better routes for synthesis of a given molecule. This is the type of problem I love to work on. Other challenges not related to chemistry that I found interesting were ones related to alternative energy and energy storage as well as oil spill clean-up. I think these problems interested me because finding solutions to these would help to make our world better. For me to get involved with problems that are outside my comfort zone, the topic must be interesting and challenging, and one that can potentially solve global problems, or improve the quality of life of many people.

The most unusual problem I took a part in was the challenge that asked to Identify Organisms from a Stream of DNA Sequences. It was outside of my professional interests but there was a super-prize of one million dollars! I suggested a principle of determining a language (used by "Google translate" and other such websites), where a language is determined on the basis of several words from the text. I suggested to use the same principle for the determination of organism species ("language") on the basis of known DNA sequences ("words"). I did not win, since the challenge required developing the source code, and I am not a programmer. But I still think that my approach can be used to solve such challenges without developing new source codes, and on the basis on existing source codes, already developed for other fields.

If you want to be a Super Solver, you have to first become a Solver and just solve a single challenge. My advice is for other Solvers out there is to take a part in the challenges that you feel that you can suggest a unique solution that will answer the company's questions. If you read a challenge description and feel that you can add value to the company and to the world, it could be your chance – my advice is to go for it. The specific approach is that your solution should be non-evident to both the company with the problem and other peer Solvers. I know that I have made a good submission when I know the direction in which other solvers will think, and then suggest something better. It was only few times, when I won challenges by suggesting something trivial. Most my winning solutions were those which were very non-standard. So, for me that "aha moment" comes when I feel that I have found something better than most other solvers may suggest to solve the challenge.

ONE SMART CROWD

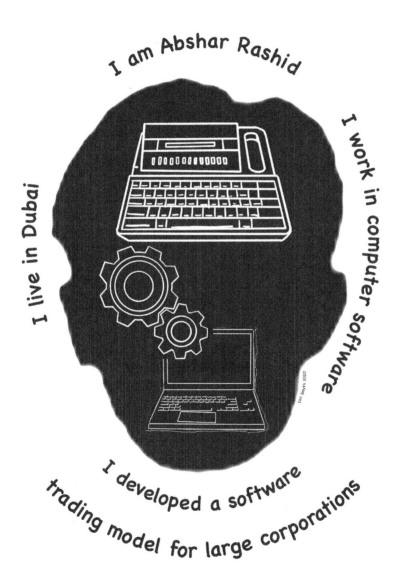

I am Abshar Rashid

I work in computer software

I live in Dubai

I developed a software trading model for large corporations

Ian Smyth 2020

My name is Abshar Rashid - "I believe, one way or another, knowledge always pays off. One might not succeed in a certain research challenge or a project at work, but the experience always transforms you into someone more skilled and knowledgeable."

Every Fortune 500 company has invested significantly to develop software ranging across the entire enterprise platform, such as process automation, financial trading, and data analysis. Some of these developments or customizations of standard platforms cost tens of millions of dollars. Typically, Fortune 500 companies hold the IP rights on the code, and have detailed system, project, as well as business process documentation. A large part of these software and business processes are in non-competitive areas and could therefore be passed on to other businesses. Ideas are required for new business models or platforms that allow simplified resale or exchange of enterprise software through third parties without incurring significant costs, legal obligations, or support.

I was interested in software development at a very young age. I designed my first software program when I was 9 years old, it was a quiz application. The interest began when my mother bought me a mid-school level toy computer that had a built in Q-Basic compiler. This toy was probably too old for me, but it attracted my curiosity. I remember I had learned the Q-Basic language all by myself using the computer manual. In fact, I was more interested in this "programming stuff" than all the other games and fun activities this toy had to offer. I still have this toy with me today; alas it no longer works despite several attempts to fix it!

I am a professional computer software engineer, with a Bachelor's degree from NED University, Pakistan. Though I have only 2 years of practical experience in the field, I have been fortunate enough to work on some very innovative and creative projects in my past jobs. Apart from software development, I have a keen interest in Management Sciences, and I am pursuing an MBA degree alongside my daytime job.

I joined the open innovation platform only a few weeks before the submission date of my awarded challenge. My reason for working on this problem was its relevance to both of my favorite fields – Software Engineering and Management Sciences. I also anticipated getting a lot of good learning and research experience, whether my solution was awarded or not. My belief is that one way or another, knowledge always pays off. You might not succeed in a certain research challenge or a project at work, but the experience always transforms you into someone more skilled and knowledgeable. For my awarded solution, I didn't get a chance to check on the internet due to the time restraint for the submission and I was short of time. I have submitted three solutions in total and have been awarded for one.

Initially, I was awed by the many scholarly profiles (PhDs or Masters) in the past winner's list. I found myself asking whether I should even attempt a solution, having such a comparatively humble experience and education. But then I just re-iterated to myself that this was a learning experience and winning was not everything. I guess it was this sincere commitment that made me come up with a solution and submission that I was confident about.

The think model is advantageous to both myself and businesses equally – companies will gain the advantage of 'outsourcing' their R&D issues to a collective talent from all around the world, while people like me get a chance to work on highly practical and intricate R&D industrial issues. It's a win win situation.

To me, innovation means to seek within. I never begin my research by searching or browsing through the internet for ideas and solutions. I do not remember having searched online for a single instance while working on this challenge. I always primarily try to come up with my own designs and my own methods, sometimes brainstorming for several straight hours. I would only search the internet if my own brainstorming failed to yield the required results.

Apart from my clear interest in software, reading and personal research are two hobbies of mine. It's difficult to balance hobbies with work, as I'm often working up to 13-hour days as I'm in the mid-level of my career. In my transit between work and home I often listen to podcasts, such as BBC's More or Less, the Freakonomics Radio, or the HBR Idea-cast. I am blessed with a very supportive wife and a son and we live happily in Dubai.

Conclusion

This book is itself a co-created product. It is borne of the stories of every day innovators from around the world. It is the creation not of the authors, but of each of those who's stories are told and contained within it. The power of the collective crowd is far greater than the sum of its parts and as businesses begin to understand and realize this, the immense opportunity that open innovation and crowdsourcing offers them will be increasingly unleashed.

We are at the early stages of a new way of innovating, of solving complex problems and of how we engage with, access and think about talent in a global economy.

For anyone who is interested in helping to change the world, one idea at a time, whether as a solution seeker or a problem solver, the opportunity is there and only you stand in the way of playing your role. We are faced with unprecedented challenges on a daily basis, together we have the capacity, capability and creativity to solve them.

#OneSmartCrowd

ILLUSTRATION AND CREATIVE DIRECTION

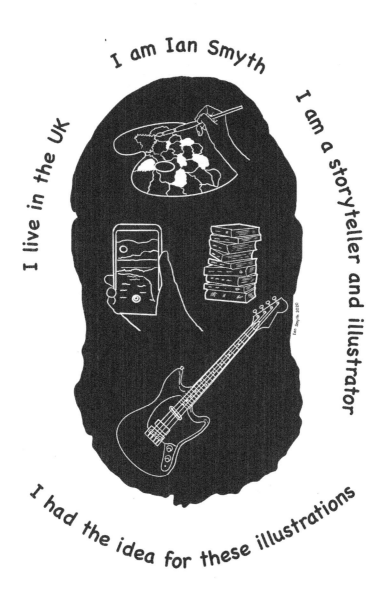

My name is Ian Smyth

I regularly create cartoons that gently poke fun at the absurdities of corporate life and innovation in particular. They help keep me sane and possibly some may reflect my own frustrations in business. It was these cartoons that led Simon Hill to approach me about working on this book. Like many innovation journeys we started off with one idea about what we were going to do and ended up with a completely different solution.

Every picture tells a story and hopefully these illustrations do the incredible people they are attempting to represent justice. I passionately believe in innovation and human potential and the stories contained within this book demonstrate both beautifully. It's been a privilege to work on bringing these amazing stories to life. Spending time with these innovators and their stories has been inspiring.

Much of the work on these illustrations was completed during long periods of Covid-19 created lockdown. This meant that my children, unable to attend school, were with me as I drew and I'd like to dedicate this to them as they inspire me each day. And to Mary without whose love and support I wouldn't be here.

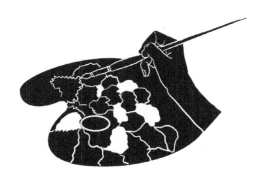

RESEARCH AND EDITORIAL

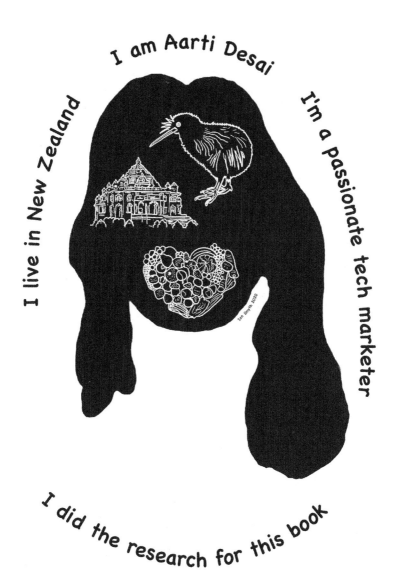

I am Aarti Desai

I'm a passionate tech marketer

I live in New Zealand

I did the research for this book

My name is Aarti Desai

The opportunity to work on this book came about in a time of change in my life. This seems fitting now, but little did I know that a short few weeks after accepting this challenge, I'd be thrown thousands of miles back to my hometown and forced into isolation and lockdown. I have worked in technology and innovation for many years, but it was over my time working at Wazoku, that I was able to truly grasp the power of open innovation and shared problem solving. Over these many months of research and editing I have become invested in these stories. As I've dug deeper into the problems and varying solutions - it really does demonstrate one incredibly smart crowd. I love the diversity in background, location, education and personality of each and every one and I'm grateful to have worked on something so significant in bringing these inspiring stories to life.

Bibliography for One Smart Crowd

HISTORIANS

Ada Lovelace
http://www.computerhistory.org/babbage/adalovelace/
https://www.theguardian.com/technology/2012/dec/10/ada-lovelace-honoured-google-doodle
http://blog.stephenwolfram.com/2015/12/untangling-the-tale-of-ada-lovelace/

Robert Evans
https://www.theaustralian.com.au/weekend-australian-magazine/reverend-robert-evans-star-gazer-and-supernova-hunter/news-story/2f09ed8311093a41795c90d36254429e
https://scribol.com/anthropology-and-history/people/the-5-most-important-amateur-scientists/.
https://www.bruderhof.com/en/voices-blog/world/encounters-supernovae-and-revival-with-reverend-robert-evans
https://csiropedia.csiro.au/evans-robert/
https://www.cabinetmagazine.org/issues/15/kastner2.php
Quote from a Book: A Short History of Nearly Everything, page 32, First Edition, Doubleday, 2003

Henrietta Swan Leavitt
https://www.famousscientists.org/henrietta-swan-leavitt/
https://www.britannica.com/biography/Henrietta-Swan-Leavitt
https://astronomy.com/news/2019/02/meet-henrietta-leavitt-the-woman-who-gave-us-a-universal-ruler
https://library.cfa.harvard.edu/phaedra/leavitt

Michael Faraday
https://www.britannica.com/biography/Michael-Faraday
http://www.bbc.co.uk/history/historic_figures/faraday_michael.shtml
https://royalsocietypublishing.org/doi/10.1098/rsta.2014.0208

Eunice Newton Foote

https://www.climate.gov/news-features/features/happy-200th-birthday-eunice-foote-hidden-climate-science-pioneer
https://time.com/5626806/eunice-foote-women-climate-science/
https://www.nytimes.com/2020/04/21/obituaries/eunice-foote-overlooked.html
https://allthatsinteresting.com/eunice-foote
https://qz.com/1277175/eunice-foote-proved-the-greenhouse-gas-effect-but-never-got-the-credit-because-of-sexism/

SUPER SOLVERS

Ed Melcarek

https://www.canadianbusiness.com/innovation/innocentive-freelancing-innovation/

SOLVERS

Ahmet Karabulut

https://www.nature.com/articles/nj7330-433a
https://www.nasa.gov/pdf/511583main_Nature_Challenges_012011.pdf
https://medlineplus.gov/druginfo/meds/a606008.html

Aaron Renn

https://www.nbcchicago.com/news/local/cta-rider-wins-5000-for-service-ideas/1863581/
https://www.govtech.com/e-government/Crowdsourcing-Helps-Chicago-Chamber-of-Commerce.html

Sandip Bharate

https://dndi.org/press-releases/2010/solver-award-dndi-challenge/
https://www.lupus.org/resources/lupus-facts-and-statistics

Sanchita Tewari

https://www.nzmp.com/global/en/news/trends-redefining-bar-market.html

https://www.globenewswire.com/news-release/2020/08/17/2079085/0/en/Worldwide-Nutritional-Bar-Industry-to-2025-Featuring-General-Mills-Halo-Foods-Kellogg-Among-Others.html

Seward Rutkove

https://www.innocentive.com/prize4life-awards-1-million-prize-for-major-milestone-in-als-research/

https://www.innocentive.com/wp-content/uploads/2019/09/InnoCentive_CDI_for_Nonprofits.pdf

https://www.forbes.com/sites/sciencebiz/2011/02/04/using-crowdsourcing-to-find-treatments-for-the-paralyzed/#429501e97e60

https://www.als.org/

Agung Nuswantoro

http://www.nbcnews.com/id/44994706/ns/technology_and_science-innovation/t/air-force-innovation-prizes-make-cents-budget-era/#.Xzm7QSgzaM8

https://www.capitalfm.co.ke/news/2012/01/dutch-win-crowdsourcing-contest-for-emergency-airdrops/

https://www.fastcompany.com/2679202/the-air-force-innovates-the-humanitarian-air-drop

https://www.nytimes.com/2016/01/20/world/middleeast/airdrops-called-too-risky-a-way-to-help-starving-syrians.html

Dr Sekhar Konjeti

https://www.coursehero.com/file/p2075mle/InnoCentive-requires-Seekers-to-pay-a-15000-posting-fee-to-publish-a-problem-on/

https://www.ideaconnection.com/problem-solver-interviews/00229-Crowdsourcing-Provides-People-with-Opportunities-to-S.html

https://www.duchenne.com/

https://www.mda.org/disease/duchenne-muscular-dystrophy/causes-inheritance

https://www.duchenneuk.org/pages/faqs/category/what-is-duchenne

Mario Alejandro Rosato
https://www.ideaconnection.com/innovative-people/mario-alejandro-rosato/recognition.html
https://www.iaa.routledge.com/authors/i16753-mario-a-rosato
https://wearesolvers.com/2016/01/19/mario-rosato-italy/
https://sustainable-technologies.eu/award-from-the-economist-to-the-best-idea-against-global-climate-change/?lang=en
https://www.un.org/en/sections/issues-depth/climate-change/
https://www.nationalgeographic.com/environment/global-warming/global-warming-overview/
https://climate.nasa.gov/evidence/

Sumit Bhardwaj
https://www.unenvironment.org/news-and-stories/press-release/un-report-time-seize-opportunity-tackle-challenge-e-waste
https://unu.edu/news/news/with-e-waste-predicted-to-double-by-2050-business-as-usual-is-not-an-option.html

Horace Lee
https://www.ninds.nih.gov/Disorders/All-Disorders/Progressive-Multifocal-Leukoencephalopathy-Information-Page
https://pubmed.ncbi.nlm.nih.gov/29620790/

Mike Cirella
https://www.ideaconnection.com/innovative-people/Mike-Cirella/problem-solver.html
ACL STATS:
https://www.ncbi.nlm.nih.gov/pmc/articles/PMC3037119/
https://www.beaumont.org/conditions/acl-tears

Amy Hong Fann
https://www.ncbi.nlm.nih.gov/pmc/articles/PMC4663196/

Trevor Rose
https://web.stanford.edu/~pdupas/BankingTheUnbanked.pdf
https://globalfindex.worldbank.org/

Giorgia Sgargetta

https://www.newsweek.com/books-crowdsourcing-and-future-business-88725
https://books.google.co.nz/books?
id=8TjiBAAAQBAJ&pg=PA322&lpg=PA322&dq=procter+and+ga
mble,
+innocentive+create+a+dishwashing+detergent+smart+enough+
to+reveal+when+exactly+the+right+amount+of+soap+has+been
+added+to+a+sink+full+of+dirty+plates.&source=bl&ots=jegyqM
yckY&sig=ACfU3U3ZciWP9suzfc7DBmNIQN9SP9SGjg&hl=en&
sa=X&ved=2ahUKEwjVh_PBsezqAhXYzzgGHTOiAeMQ6AEwD
3oECAoQAQ#v=onepage&q=procter%20and%20gamble%2C%
20innocentive%20create%20a%20dishwashing%20detergent%
20smart%20enough%20to%20reveal%20when%20exactly%20t
he%20right%20amount%20of%20soap%20has%20been%20ad
ded%20to%20a%20sink%20full%20of%20dirty%20plates.&f=fal
se
https://www.statista.com/statistics/1078347/dishwashing-liquid-market-value-worldwide/

Mark Hudson
https://blogs.sap.com/2009/07/13/meet-mark-hudson-solver-scn-member/
https://blogs.sap.com/2009/05/12/explorerpolestar-contest-winners-announced/
https://translate.google.com/translate?hl=en&sl=zh-CN&u=https://www.euroeins.com/blog/2009/07/09/im-a-solver-mark-hudson&prev=search&pto=aue
Madhavi Muranjan
https://www.ninds.nih.gov/Disorders/All-Disorders/Progressive-Multifocal-Leukoencephalopathy-Information-Page
https://pubmed.ncbi.nlm.nih.gov/29620790/

James Mitchell
https://industrialecart.com/blog/what-are-industrial-lubricants-and-their-types/

Adam Rivers
https://books.google.co.nz/books?
id=YwZeCwAAQBAJ&pg=PT126&lpg=PT126&dq=adam+rivers+
innocentive+milkshake&source=bl&ots=0rfMGi4SJr&sig=ACfU3
U1yiE2rpDlp-
qg2MgExZEhYcB0EkQ&hl=en&sa=X&ved=2ahUKEwipttHPyp7r
AhXn63MBHVkCA0kQ6AEwAnoECAoQAQ#v=onepage&q=ada
m%20rivers%20innocentive%20milkshake&f=false

Gregg Micinilio
https://www.ctpost.com/local/article/Trumbull-man-designs-low-
cost-water-filtration-1023697.php
https://ec.europa.eu/clima/change/consequences_en
https://www.un.org/en/sections/issues-depth/climate-change/

Vicky Hunt
https://www.sciencedirect.com/topics/veterinary-science-and-
veterinary-medicine/feline-odontoclastic-resorptive-
lesion#:~:text=Feline%20odontoclastic%20resorptive%20lesions
%20(FORLs)
%20are%20one%20of%20the%20most,to%20eat%20in%20affe
cted%20cats

Jose Luis Susa Rincon
https://ka-ge.facebook.com/notes/innocentive-open-innovation-
network/im-a-solver-jose-luis-susa-rincon/10150148776699181/
https://www.pewsocialtrends.org/2015/12/17/parenting-in-
america/

Sheeraj Pawar
https://www2.deloitte.com/content/dam/insights/us/articles/
4331_Deloitte-City-Mobility-Index/
Mumbai_GlobalCityMobility_WEB.pdf
https://indianexpress.com/article/india/mumbai-suburban-
network-98-stations-dangerous-to-differently-abled-senior-
citizens-4538864/

Garima Kaul

https://www.researchgate.net/publication/
258131968_Points_to_Consider_in_Defining_Region_for_a_Mul
tiregional_Clinical_Trial_Defining_Region_Work_Stream_in_Ph
RMA_MRCT_Key_Issue_Team

Bodgan and Stephanie Yamkovenko

http://visualoop.com/blog/1946/the-economist-nielsen-data-
visualization-contest-winners
http://stephanieyamkovenko.com/pdf/dataviz1.pdf
https://www.rit.edu/showcase/index.php?id=186
https://syciphers.wordpress.com/2012/12/06/we-won-the-
economist-data-visualization-challenge/
https://www.innocentive.com/winner-revealed-the-economist-
nielsen-data-visualization-challenge/

Corrine Le Buhan

https://www.ipstudies.ch/about/corinne-le-buhan-phd/
https://www.ipstudies.ch/2011/09/news_humanpotential2011/
https://www.innocentive.com/the-economist-and-innocentive-
announce-human-potential-challenge-winner-and-mark-one-
year-anniversary-of-the-partnership/
https://www.ipstudies.ch/wordpress/wp-content/uploads/2011/09/
CreativeSharingIndex_Distribution1.pdf
https://www.businesswire.com/news/home/20110913006664/en/
The-Economist-and-InnoCentive-Announce-Human-Potential-
Challenge-Winner-and-Mark-One-Year-Anniversary-of-the-
Partnership
https://ourworldindata.org/human-development-index

Zacary Brown

https://books.google.co.nz/books?
id=qGW1DwAAQBAJ&pg=PA23&lpg=PA23&dq=Zacary+Brown
+radio+operaor&source=bl&ots=XuKIbcJJ9I&sig=ACfU3U21PLc
JYFjvmcrUHdPQYxxsMMnh-
A&hl=en&sa=X&ved=2ahUKEwj31pC1__XoAhWCxzgGHRLKB
60Q6AEwAHoECAoKw#v=onepage&q=Zacary%20Brown%20
radio%20operaor&f=false
https://yourstory.com/2008/09/solar-powered-wireless-router-
offers-opportunities-in-technology

https://www.ideaconnection.com/open-innovation-success/Solar-Powered-Wireless-Router-00053.html

Andrew Deonarine
https://www.bctechnology.com/news/2010/9/9/UBC-Medical-Student-Wins-21st-Century-Cyber-Schools-Challenge.cfm
https://www.innocentive.com/the-economist-and-innocentive-announce-a-winner-in-the-21st-century-cyber-schools-challenge/
https://ourworldindata.org/global-education
https://www.globalpartnership.org/results/education-data-highlights
https://acei-global.blog/2014/03/06/15-facts-on-education-in-developing-countries/

Adriaan Mol
https://www.worldvision.org/clean-water-news-stories/global-water-crisis-facts

Hannah Safford
https://www.usbr.gov/newsroom/stories/detail.cfm?RecordID=65303
https://www.statista.com/statistics/192838/revenue-from-us-wastewater-treatment-since-2000/
https://www.brookings.edu/research/in-times-of-drought-nine-economic-facts-about-water-in-the-united-states/

Patrick Fuller
https://ideascale.com/wp-content/uploads/2014/12/Network-Intelligence1.pdf
https://www.linkedin.com/in/patrickemmettfuller/
https://www.conservationmagazine.org/2012/06/the-best-ideas-money-can-buy/
https://www.ncbi.nlm.nih.gov/pmc/articles/PMC3156687/

Aake Staahl
https://edition.cnn.com/2010/US/05/15/oil.spill.dispersants/index.html

Ammanamanchi Radhakrishna
https://www.fightaging.org/archives/2010/08/seeking-a-way-to-break-down-glucosepane/
https://www.innocentive.com/innocentive-and-sens-foundation-seek-innovative-ideas-to-help-reverse-age-related-illnesses/

Ruby Grewal
https://www.popsci.com/diy/article/2012-08/challenge-answered/
https://www.avastin.com/hcp.html
https://www.cancer.net/navigating-cancer-care/how-cancer-treated/personalized-and-targeted-therapies/angiogenesis-and-angiogenesis-inhibitors-treat-cancer

Manish M. Pande
https://www.statista.com/outlook/20020000/100/soft-drinks/worldwide

Thomas Stowe
https://www.olympiceyewear.com/blog/great-facts-about-polycarbonate-the-wonder-plastic/
https://www.acplasticsinc.com/informationcenter/r/what-is-polycarbonate

David Bradin
https://www.linkedin.com/in/david-bradin-9945641/
https://www.nexsenpruet.com/professionals/david-s-bradin
http://www.mavericksynfuels.com/about-us/management-team/
https://www.ideaconnection.com/open-innovation-success/An-Acid-Synthesis-Method-00064.html

Samuel Pena-Llopis
https://www.researchgate.net/publication/6843266_Deaths_from_pesticide_poisoning_A_global_response
https://bmcpublichealth.biomedcentral.com/articles/10.1186/1471-2458-7-357
https://pubmed.ncbi.nlm.nih.gov/10230392/

John Davis
https://www.ideaconnection.com/open-innovation-success/
Open-Innovation-Exxon-Valdez-Cleanup-00030.html
https://www.youtube.com/watch?v=5_ucQKWmxdk
https://www.youtube.com/watch?v=wW-O86BDRQU
https://www.history.com/topics/1980s/exxon-valdez-oil-spill

Anon
https://cleanahull.com/ultrasonic-antifouling/marine-bio-fouling-explained/
http://issg.org/pdf/publications/GISP/Resources/BiofoulingGuidelines.pdf

Abshar Rashid
https://wearesolvers.com/2016/01/18/abshar-rashid/
https://ar-ar.facebook.com/note.php?note_id=433916409180
https://jehanara.wordpress.com/2010/08/09/abshar-rashid-solves-a-problem-on-innocentive/
https://www.youtube.com/watch?v=nsz2B_Wj1DM&ab_channel=Daydreamer.Pictures
https://fortune.com/global500/
https://corporatefinanceinstitute.com/resources/careers/companies/fortune-500/

Printed in Great Britain
by Amazon